D1566042

THE STATE OF THE UNION OF EUROPE

Some Titles of Related Interest

DANZIN
Science and the Second Renaissance of Europe

DIWAN and LIVINGSTON
Alternative Development Strategies and Appropriate Technology

FRY
Industrial Democracy and Labour Market Policy in Sweden

GVISHIANI
Science, Technology and Global Problems

KERR
The Common Market and How It Works

NILLSSON
The State of the Planet

PECCEI
The Human Quality

POWER
Migrant Workers in Western Europe and the United States

SHANKS
European Social Policy Today and Tomorrow

THOMAS and WIONCZEK
Integration of Science and Technology with Development

THE STATE
OF THE UNION OF EUROPE

Report of the CADMOS Group to the European People

Edited by

DENIS DE ROUGEMONT

Translated by
V. IONESCU

PERGAMON PRESS
OXFORD · NEW YORK · TORONTO · SYDNEY · PARIS · FRANKFURT

U.K.	Pergamon Press Ltd., Headington Hill Hall, Oxford OX3 0BW, England
U.S.A.	Pergamon Press Inc., Maxwell House, Fairview Park, Elmsford, New York 10523, U.S.A.
CANADA	Pergamon of Canada, Suite 104, 150 Consumers Road, Willowdale, Ontario M2J 1P9, Canada
AUSTRALIA	Pergamon Press (Aust.) Pty. Ltd., P.O. Box 544, Potts Point, N.S.W. 2011, Australia
FRANCE	Pergamon Press SARL, 24 rue des Ecoles, 75240 Paris, Cedex 05, France
FEDERAL REPUBLIC OF GERMANY	Pergamon Press GmbH, 6242 Kronberg-Taunus, Pferdstrasse 1, Federal Republic of Germany

First edition 1979

British Library Cataloguing in Publication Data

State of the union of Europe.
1. European Communities
I. Rougemont, Denis de
II. CADMOS Group
382'.9142'09047 HC241.2 79-40100
ISBN 0 08 024483-1 (Hardcover)
ISBN 0 08 024476-9 (Flexicover)

Printed in Great Britain by
Biddles Ltd, Guildford, Surrey

Contents

	Foreword	vii
	Introduction	1
1	*The Economy*	25
2	*Energy*	41
3	*Environment*	49
4	*The Regions*	59
5	*European Defence*	73
6	*Europe and the Third World*	81
7	*Programme for the Europeans*	87
	Appendix I	93
	Appendix II	95
	Appendix III	97

Foreword

SET up in 1976 on the initiative of the CENTRE EUROPÉEN DE LA CULTURE (Geneva)

THE CADMOS GROUP

is composed of about thirty members from nine Western European countries—economists, ecologists, educators, political scientists, philosophers, sociologists. Its general objective was to a pluridisciplinarian reflection on the problems and the responsibilities of Europeans today faced with the necessity to unite, with the values which promote this union, and with the role it must play in the world.

The Group's first common task was to draw up a

Report to the European People

ON THE STATE OF THE UNION OF EUROPE

(in the absence of any high legal body entrusted by a Constitution to do this).

In plenary or partial sessions, the Group discussed texts proposed by several of its members on the important themes for this year.

It is the synthesis of these discussions which is today submitted to the European public.

The following members of the CADMOS Group have contributed to the Introduction and the seven chapters of this first report with texts, information, arguments and constructive criticism:

FRANCOIS BONDY	Author and journalist, Zürich.
EMILIO FONTELA	Professor, University of Geneva.
JACQUES FREYMOND	Prof. Institut Universitaire des Hautes Etudes Internationales, Geneva.
ORIO GIARINI	Economist, Geneva.

vii

EDWARD GOLDSMITH	Director, *The Ecologist,* London.
OTTO HIERONYMI	Institut Batelle, Geneva.
ALEXANDER KING	Economist, Founding Member of The Club of Rome, Paris.
FERDINAND KINSKY	General Director of the CIFE, Nice.
PATRICIA MAYO	Author and sociologist, Cornwall.
CHARLES RICQ	Sociologist, Geneva.
HENRI SCHWAMM	Professor, Institut Universitaire d'Études Européennes, Geneva.
MANFRED SIEBKER	Physicist and sociologist, Brussels.
ROBERT TRIFFIN	Economist, Professor, Yale University.

The final editor, DENIS DE ROUGEMONT, President of the European Cultural Centre, assumes entire responsibility for the arrangement of the contributions so generously put at his disposal by the members of the Group and for the formulation of its conclusions.

The European Cultural Centre thanks the European Cultural Foundation (Amsterdam) which made possible the meetings of the CADMOS Group and the preparation of this first Report.

Introduction

Which Europe?

Europeans, it would seem, do not think *badly* of the Europe which is being shaped; in fact they seem to be sympathetic towards it. But the question is how often do they think of it? The abolition of the last customs duties between the nine countries of the Common Market on 1 July 1977 took place almost unnoticed. Yet it was the first achievement of Jean Monnet's grand design, the inspirer of the economic Europe, his first objective to be fully reached.

Must one conclude from this that 'Europe is no longer interesting', as most of our newspapers have been repeating for some years, while at the same time they devote more and more space in their columns to it? Or rather that the Europe which really *interests* today's Europeans is not primarily the Europe of the economy and of free trade but rather that of the opportunities life offers, the opportunities for peace and for the upholding of freedom, that is, of the progress of civic responsibilities?

'Europe is finished', stated the Press. Or at least this is what it was saying before the election of the European Parliament was announced. Here are some samples of headlines which appeared in the main French, Swiss, Belgian, Italian, German and British newspapers from 1974 to 1976:

On Europe in general: *L'Europe agonise—L'Europe à la dérive—L'Europe se meurt—L'Europe, c'est fini.*

On the activities of the Nine: *L'Europe verte écartelée—Europe Agrarpolitik—wer kann das noch verstehen?—Les Neuf divisés sur leur politique énergétique—Conseil Européen: l'enlisement—Les Neuf ont étalé divergences et absence de volonté politique—Fallito del vertico europeo—L'anarchie de la CEE—Europa auf der Flucht—Europe passes a milestone in lagging drive for unity.*

Reading these titles, one wonders which Europe they are talking about? What is this Europe which, according to them, is dying?

If it is the 'Europe of the Nine' they should call it by its name: the European Economic Community, or the Common Market. And they should then try to show seriously either the reasons for its relative failure or in what and why the institution has failed and how saying that 'Brussels is finished' is the equivalent of saying that 'Europe is dying'. This is far from self-evident.

If it is the Europe of States—more or less 'united' or 'confederated'—which ministers have constantly told us for the last 30 years is an urgent necessity, the statement is false: this Europe cannot be dying because it has never existed, and it is doubtful whether it will ever see the light of day so long as the States refuse to yield up any of their national sovereignty.

Are they then speaking of the real Europe, that of living Europeans, of their cultures and of their hopes? But then how can they speak so calmly, without the slightest emotion in their voices and sometimes even with a hint of resigned complacency, even of sly jubilation—how can they announce and accept that all that be lost—*as if all that were not ourselves?*

It seems that to the journalists who wrote the headlines, the 'Europe which is dying' is something which does not concern them personally at all. They speak of it as one speaks of far-off disasters, of the death which only comes to others. But are they fully aware of the ineluctable fact that they themselves will suffer the concrete fate of Europe, regardless of whether they are for or against, of the Left or of the Right, pro-European or nationalist? Their dramatic statements reflect far less the experience which our continent has undergone than a general mental confusion as to the true nature of the Europe of which they are speaking. Is this 'Europe' to be nothing more than a market? An economic community? An alliance of sovereign States? Should it not be, on the contrary, the totality of Europeans, of their countries, problems, memories and hopes, moulded by twelve centuries of common history and three millenniums of intermingled cultures, from the Iberian Peninsula to the Baltic States, from Scotland to the Balkans, and from Greece to Scandinavia?

Purpose of this Report

It must be understood that the Report will speak of the living Europe, that of the Europeans, not of the States; that of the citizens, not of the bureaucrats; that of the vital problems of all the inhabitants of our 'tip of Asia', not only of those of the nine countries whose governments are associated together in Brussels in order to harmonise their industrial and commercial policies.

It will situate the Europe of today first of all in *world realities, then in Western realities.*

It will go on to try first to formulate the *problems of the century which, by their nature and by their size, are seen to be insoluble within the framework of the national sovereignties and which call therefore for continental or regional solutions of union, above and beyond our Nation-States.*

1. Europe and the World

Problems Which No State Can Solve Alone

Europe's situation in the world today is marked by a violent contrast: there is a *population explosion* in the Third World, especially in South-East Asia and in certain parts of Latin America, while in the industrialised countries of Europe the birth rate is falling, sometimes approaching zero growth. (The same phenomenon is noticeable in the Soviet Union, where the birth rate in the Russian part remains low while that of the Asiatic Republics is constantly increasing. In a few decades the Mohammedans and Asians will be in the majority in the USSR.)

This is what indeed could change dramatically the 'traditional' balance between Europe and the rest of the world.

The *food requirements* of the Third World will increase in a way which will inevitably lead to disaster in many cases. For example, the demographers of Bangladesh forecast a death rate through famine of more than 20 million per annum in the eighties until the excess population is corrected 'by nature'—unless an enormous quantity of food can be obtained from abroad. Some of this can be supplied by the United States and by them alone. But this will be at the cost of a rapid expansion of their agricultural production which is particularly wasteful of energy and devastating for the environment, and so vulnerable.

The American monopoly of the world food supplies is approaching a situation comparable to the Arab oil monopoly. It will not be easy for the United States never to use this advantage for political ends in that the USSR will possibly remain the largest customer for American wheat in years of bad harvests. For such years will become more and more frequent if the climatologists are right. We must therefore expect the economic and political power of the United States to become ever more dominant.

In Europe, too, *the forecast deterioration in the climate* could bring serious consequences as regards food stocks. Recent research would seem to show that the years 1935 to 1965 of the century marked an optimum in the history of agriculture. We must prepare ourselves for a period of alternation, for at least one hundred years, between excessive heat and cold, between drought and floods. This is still only a hypothesis, but what does seem certain is that technological progress has made modern society, particularly its agriculture, far more vulnerable to climatic variations.

Another consequence of the growing demographic discrepancies between the West and the Third World is the increasingly strong migratory pressure of the Third World on the developed countries. This has already begun with the influx of Indians and Pakistanis into Britain and with the illegal immigration of the Mexicans into the United States, which is estimated at six millions.

The proportion of Whites with a high standard of living will diminish ever more rapidly in relation to the population of the Third World, and their average age will be older. The growth of the world population and of its 'needs' per head in terms of energy and raw materials—in an aggressive and wasteful Western-type economy—cannot fail to have very severe repercussions for all the people of Europe.

In fact, having been the first to launch the industrial revolution, we have already made great inroads into our resources and we can no longer count upon automatic access to the greater part of our external sources of supply. The oil crisis in 1973 showed how vulnerable our economy had become to remote political events over which we no longer had any control, and which find us disarmed in that we have no plan of mutual first aid, no common medium- or long-term policy and very little common will to co-operate, very little wisdom.

In these circumstances union is vital. Without it our countries run the immediate risk of being infiltrated, then invaded, colonised materially and morally, one after the other—but fully independent—one from the other!

All these tensions, heavy with latent conflicts, threaten all the Europeans in their living standards first of all, then in their political independence, and, finally, in their survival pure and simple.

For it is obvious that none of our countries can master these dangers alone. The solutions called for by planetary or continental threats clearly go beyond the individual capacity of any one of our States as much for their decisions as for their implementation. *Only the Union of Europeans* will have any real chance of bringing about appreciable results on the world scale.

Demographic imbalances; social and cultural disintegration; shortages and famine; foreign monopolies leading to various forms of enslavement, economic, then political; crisis of civilisation leading to incalculable disasters if we continue in the same direction and at the same rhythm—the cumulation of these physical, material, alimentary, climatic and economic factors—urgent, immediately sensitive and literally vital as they may be—is far from taking into account the whole reality which the inhabitants of the European peninsula must face today.

All the lucid observers of our age have felt it. We all repeat that we must give another direction to the 'development' of our society and to reconsider the definition of what we Europeans were the first and for a long time the only ones to call 'Progress'.

Happiness, the health of mankind and, quite simply, its material well-being—are they really linked to growth of the GNP and of the use of energy as capitalists and communists, socialists and liberals have maintained for the last century? But if this is going to lead us from crisis to crisis and from shortages and famine to the final disaster of nuclear war, is it not time to chart a new course? To revise the dogmas of material progress of the unlimited growth of everything and anything, of salvation by quantity regardless of quality which cannot be a matter of book-keeping? Let us ask then who can conceive, wish and bring about this change of direction.

It is not likely to be the Third World: its dominant passion—or in any case the passion of its dominant classes—appears to be to reproduce within itself the very causes of our crisis: it accuses us of trying to frustrate it whenever we attempt to warn it. (It wants not merely our motor-cars but also our bottlenecks and even our oil shortages, which seem to demand nuclear plants.)

It is not likely to be the USSR which wants to 'catch up with America' and continues to believe, for the most part, that the bigger it is the better.

There remains then our 'old Europe': Europe was the first to invent Progress, then the first to become aware of its mistakes in direction. It would thus seem natural that it would also be the first which could change direction and rectify the conception of 'progress' which she launched upon the whole world and which the most 'traditional' societies adopt or acquiesce in today. Will Europe fail in this world mission? Can it do so without betraying the grounds of its existence and abdicating, together with its responsibilities, its liberties?

The Two Europes

Here we ask the fundamental question: Which Europe? For there are two.

History shows us the birth in Greece of the autonomous City States, of a Europe of dialogue, of civic solidarity, of reason and of measure, of critical spirit and Socratic tolerance.

But history shows us also the birth in Imperial Rome of what was to become the Europe of dictatorships, of levelling collectivist regulation of the *raison d'État,* generally contrary to reason and of the 'right place' reserved, according to Lenin, for the political opposition, that is, prison.

The first Europe created and nourished the ideas of liberty and of responsibility in the community, of sworn faith and of federal pact, then of the international, of internationalism and of arbitration, lastly of European federation. It is a Europe of active citizens.

The second Europe is made up of passive subjects. It has fallen back on the Roman idea that 'to die for one's country (in reality for the State) is the most beautiful, the most enviable fate'. This Europe is that of etatist nationalisms, of their 'glorious' wars, of their revolutions, of fascism of the Left and then of the Right, and of 'technological imperatives' in the service of 'absolute national sovereignties'.

Now today it is the second Europe which is opposed to the federal union of our peoples, the only hope before us. Unfortunately, it is this second Europe that the Third World copies with passion.

To Imitate Europe?

'Everything came to Europe and everything came from it; or almost everything' wrote Paul Valéry. This is true but in that 'everything' there is perhaps as much evil as good. The civilisation born in Europe—rational, critical, liberal, aimed at liberating the individual—has not been able to prevent the totalitarian State, that is everything that denies reason, critical spirit and personal liberty. It is no less true that the civilisation born in Europe went round the world, that it was the first to do so and will for long remain the only one to have done so. It has been copied by the majority and practically by all the new States, born of decolonisation between 1946 and 1976.

But can one describe as 'decolonisation' a process which perpetuates at one and the same time the frontiers drawn upon the map in the offices of our capitals of colonising countries and our most characteristic superstitions, among which is the idea of material Progress, the ideal of the centralised Nation-State and of its 'absolute sovereignty' and, lastly and above all, the equation of 'The happiness of man equals growth in public and private expenditure (or GNP), waste of energy, terrorism, suicides, neuroses, drugs, cancer[1] and, finally, the atomic bomb'?

The fact is that it is easier to copy the caricatures rather than the models, the vices rather than the virtues, the weapons of war rather than the procedures of peace. It is easier to appropriate the prescriptions of arrogant nationalism than those of responsible federalism.

[1] Probability of cancer in Europe: in 1900, 3%; in 1978, 33%. These figures correspond by and large to that of the increase (not counting inflation) of the GNP.

Easier to decree the single party than to win the moral consensus of the citizens. Easier to exercise dictatorship than to promote and to educate liberties, self-regulated by the sense of civic responsibilities. The totalitarian State will always be easier than the democratic community. Death is easier than life.

Nearly eighty new States have proclaimed their independence since the end of the Second World War. And all have adopted the European model of the centralised State with unlimited sovereignty. Because all want at any price to copy the structures of the Napoleonic State and the armaments of nuclear imperialism, this division of the world into sovereign States must inevitably lead to a general war. It could well be the last because it will destroy the very bases of every war: human societies and their civilisations.

The Chances for Europe

What remains for Europe in these circumstances?

The United States possesses the technological means of material above all destructive power combined with the principles of an idealism which claims to be Christian. The USSR possesses the means of a quantitative gigantism and of an ideology which claims to be Marxist.

What remains peculiar to Europe? The Greek sense of measure, the Roman sense of law, the Germanic sense of the community of free men, the Celtic sense of spiritual adventure—not to speak of that vague nostalgia or Christian remorse, because of the love banned in public or private relations, but expressed most preferably in terms of the claims of justice and equality.

These trumps are very strong but we never play them. Because all our governments and most of the great parties of the Right or the Left (resembling in this the Third World) mostly obey—not in their speeches but in the facts—the principles and values of the second Europe, that of national sovereignties and material power, as opposed to the first Europe, that of the international solidarity and of the responsible liberty of the citizens. The division of the European continent into Nation-States, which are inevitably rivals, foils every attempt at free co-operation across the national frontiers, those 'scars of history' drawn despite reality by the hazards of wars and treaties.

The division of the continent into some thirty 'absolute national sovereignties' is the sole explanation why the reasons for union described above and which none of our governments can any longer ignore have up to now remained almost totally inoperative. It is only together that we can get out of it. We cannot survive the crises by confining ourselves to opposing to them our vaunted 'national sovereignties', that is rhetoric. The choice is a simple one: either we perish one by one or we survive federated.

2. Europe and the West

This being the state of Europe in the world, what is its standing in the West?

Most Europeans have the discouraging impression that they are being 'crushed' between the super-powers of the East and of the West. This feeling, which is not justified by facts and figures, is nevertheless a reflection of the divided state of the continent. If we felt that we were Europeans, members of a federal community of around 383 million inhabitants in the West (until the 128 or so millions of the East European satellites could rejoin us if they wanted to, not to speak of the Baltic countries), we could look without excessive fear at the 220 million Americans and the 256 million inhabitants of the USSR: when these super-powers are added together they do not add up to our figure. But we feel primarily and often exclusively that we are part of one country which, even if it is still called a 'power', carries no weight when compared with the great continental unions of the USSR and the United States. It is obvious that the number of inhabitants does not have the last word about the power or the happiness of a people, but if it is true that we are over-inclined to judge according to quantities, this example shows clearly that our present defeatism is only justified by our state of division, by our refusal to federate.

Behind our exaggeratedly pessimistic representations and in the expectation of a reunion of the peoples which have been Europeanised for a thousand years, what are the actual realities?

Between the United States and the USSR, the state of Europe looks very unhealthy and riven with intolerable injustices.

It is not healthy that our economy and our currencies remain at the mercy of a manipulation of the exchange rate of the dollar or of the inflation exported notably by the American economy as a result of the Vietnam War.

It is not healthy that what is called the security of Europe appears to be guaranteed by the presence of a few American divisions in the German Federal Republic, not by the union of the European forces and wills.

It is not healthy that Europeans should shelter under the American nuclear 'umbrella' in order to avoid facing up to their responsibilities, above all to avoid the recognition that these can only be assumed together.

It is not healthy that the abusive survival (in Europe as well as in Latin America) of military or clerical dictatorial, openly anti-democratic regimes should be able to depend on 'American aid'.

But, on the other hand, it is not right that eight European countries—Poland, the German Democratic Republic, Czechoslovakia, Hungary, Yugoslavia, Romania, Bulgaria and Albania—should be deprived of the right to decide about their eventual federation with the West of the continent. It is not right that as soon as they show a predilection, no matter how timid, for democracy, they should be invaded by the Russians. It is not right that at Yalta the peoples of south-east Europe should have been 'shared' and 'allotted' among the super-powers in protectorates, satellites, zones of limited sovereignty, etc., as the tribes of black Africa were by the Berlin Conference of 1885.

What is right, human and urgent is to work for and to desire the federation of Europe, which is the only way to withstand the economic or political grip of the super-powers.

3. Evolution of the Motives for Union

To Go Beyond National Sovereignties

In 1944 the delegates of the resistance movements of nine countries (including Germany and Italy) met secretly in Geneva on four occasions and drew up a common manifesto calling for a federal union of Europe at the end of hostilities. It was time, they said, to 'go beyond the dogma of absolute national sovereignty'. Only a federation of the democracies could prevent a new Franco-German war, like those which had sparked off two world wars in the space of one generation.

And this was the dominant theme of the first congresses of European federalists once hostilities had ended from 1945 to 1947.

In 1946 the leagues of notables or of young militants from all classes—men and women, politicians, economists, trade unionists and industrialists—had recommended measures for a 'stronger union' of our countries aimed at the economic reconstruction of the continent. The Marshall Plan in 1947 brought them powerful means to achieve this. Some, drawn mostly from the resistance, stated expressly that they were federalists. Others, in order not to upset the established values, described themselves as 'unionists'.

The two trends met at the Congress of Europe in The Hague (May 1948) under the honorary presidency of Churchill, who was present and active. They proposed the creation of a Council of Europe endowed with an 'Assembly in which would be represented all the live forces of all our nations'.

This led to the creation, at the beginning of March 1949, of the Council of Europe in Strasbourg. Was Europe born in nine months? Certainly not: its Assembly was to be purely consultative and composed of deputies appointed by the various national Parliaments, not elected by the people. The federalist drive had been broken.

In 1949 Jean Monnet inspired and Robert Schuman realised a plan which seemed to guarantee materially the union of Franco-German interests. This was the European Coal and Steel Community (ECSC) which was created in Luxembourg in 1950.

As for the economic trend, it ended in the Treaty of Rome (1957) bringing the gradual institutionalisation of a common market which today is called European Community but which in fact is still only a grouping of the governments of nine European countries out of thirty countries (including the countries of the East) which try to enforce the 'communitarian' rules in the economic sector. Its aims? To support the growth of the economy in general and the expansion of the great enterprises.

As for the motif of the defence of the continent (which did not appear as such during the creative and militant period of the great

European Congresses from 1947 to 1950),[1] it animated the project of a European Defence Community (the EDC) presented by France to five other countries of the ECSC and immediately accepted by them, but finally rejected by the French members of parliament, the nationalists and the Communists combined.

The failure of the EDC marked the first defeat of the European idea as a policy of civilisation beyond the ideological and partisan stereotypes inherited from the materialistic nineteenth century and its specific superstitions like Science, Progress, Nationalism, and the unlimited Growth of everything.

This political defeat caused a lively reaction: to 'restart the building of Europe' but only in the economic sphere.

This was the cause of the flagging enthusiasm, the disappointment and the disaffection in the ranks of the young federalists.

On the one hand, the youth of today are no longer aware of what the Franco-German antagonism meant: the motive of preventing its return has therefore lost much of its force. On the other, one can see among older people a very marked return of chauvinism and of mutual suspicion, and this even in the political circles which, on the subject of Europe and of the Six, declared, 25 years ago (on the German side): 'This little Europe is simply a great France' (Socialist leader Kurt Schumacher); and on the French side: 'This Europe is a great Germany' (Ex-President of the Council, Edouard Daladier). Nationalists and communists today denounce 'the political danger of the Paris-Bonn axis' or, worse still, that of 'the Germano-American Europe'. These phantasmagoria can make one forget—it is perhaps their only explanation—that security in Europe is not guaranteed by any of our countries, neither for itself or for its neighbours and still less by the calculations of an 'American administration' which the Pentagon computers could one fine day urge to leave us to get on with it alone.

When the proposal that there should be direct elections to the European Parliament was announced, the Press once more spoke of a new start. There are two reasons why the expression does not bear scrutiny.

[1] Federalist Congress of Montreux, 1947. Congress of Europe in The Hague, 1948. Economic Congress at Westminster, 1948. Political Congress in Brussels, 1949. European Conference on Culture, Lausanne, 1949.

(1) The too oft repeated announcement of a new start evokes breathlessness rather than a new impetus.

(2) The election of the European Parliament by universal suffrage, late as it may be, is only the follow-up of the European policy of the fifties, anxious not to infringe in any way sacrosanct national sovereignties while naturally in favour of the formation of a European Opinion.

This policy is actually blocked in Brussels as well as in Strasbourg by the national sovereignties to which all the parties have renewed their unconditional and pious allegiance in the debates in the national parliaments. It would be unreasonable to hope that the federalist movements, so dynamic at the end of the war, would succeed in mobilising, in support of Brussels and Strasbourg, more than the nostalgia of the militants.

4. What Our Disunited States Can No Longer Accomplish

But here at the nadir of the movement for a united Europe completely new motivations, which 10 years ago could not be foreseen in a few months, became of first-rank importance.

The two single causes able to mobilise several times in a single summer—that of 1977—tens or hundreds of thousands of militants were that of the *ecology* and that of the *regions*. Now both these causes were linked from the outset to the cause of the *federal union* of our people. The green front, local and regional autonomies, communities of all vocations—these are the names and the symbols of what today attracts and animates across our countries the civic sense of the young, their anger, their hopes.

This new European wave is motivated by a Western juncture extending from San Francisco to Vladivostok. Moreover, by a global juncture for it is from the whole world that the great warnings come which tell us to unite, that is *to survive together or to perish separately.*

In the present state of the division of Europe into twenty-eight sovereign States which, in order better to affirm their sovereignty, refuse to federate in the West or which, having in the East only a controlled sovereignty, cannot renounce it, it must be agreed that the Europeans, if they rely solely on their national forces, cannot accomplish any of the tasks which the government of a nation is normally expected to do and which are the reason for its existence.

In the present state of division, our 'sovereignties' cannot in effect:

— resist economic colonisation by the United States;
— repel a military intervention from the East;
— fight against inflation without increasing unemployment;
— reduce unemployment without increasing inflation;
— maintain the value of their currency;
— deal with their needs in the sphere of energy without threatening the environment and using the police to prevent the exercise of democratic rights;
— prevent or cure the pollution of the lakes, rivers and seas;
— come to the aid of the Third World in its struggle against famine and its passion for copying and appropriating the very causes of our own crisis;
— guarantee the necessary supplies of raw materials and combustible energy producers;
— nor, finally, make good use of the Continent's own resources in capital, equipment, technology, competence and creativity.

Without concertation at the continental level and common institutions of the federal type, our Nation-States, entrenched in their national sovereignties, cannot escape in the coming decades the dangers which we listed at the start, some of which are irreversible and therefore mortal, as we have seen.

Europe must unite if it is to survive.

It must survive in order not to drag mankind with it in its fall.

5. What Has Been Achieved So Far

The Council of Europe

Such being the reasons for uniting, what have been the measures taken to respond to them at the level of governmental or private political action?

The first European organism, created on the proposal of the Congress of Europe which met in The Hague in May 1948, was to bring a

'European Assembly in which would be represented the live forces in all our nations'.

In fact the *Council of Europe,* inaugurated in 1949, was only given a Consultative Assembly composed of non-elected members, appointed by the parliaments of the Member-States and chosen from among their number. It soon became resigned to being nothing more than a forum for the exchange of political and social ideas, a role which it has continued to play with distinction but without the slightest popular impact.

It is important that this Consultative Assembly should not be confused with the *Parliament of the EEC,* created by the Treaty of Rome, which also meets in Strasbourg and for which the States have decided to hold direct elections in June 1979 in the nine countries of the present Community, in accordance with the Treaty of Rome, which was signed in 1957.

Once the Parliament has been elected, the Consultative Assembly of the Council of Europe will keep as its main justification—and possibly its only one—the constitution of the indispensable link between the Member-States of the economic Community and the other democracies of Western Europe—from the Iberian peninsula to Austria, passing through Switzerland, and from Scandinavia to Greece, Malta and Cyprus.

More original and of more easily measurable efficiency are two other activities of the Council of Europe which are practically unknown to the public at large. One was laid down from the beginning: *The European Commission for Human Rights and its Court;* the other which developed during the sixties: *The European Conference of Local and Regional Powers.*

On the first, Chancellor Helmut Schmidt, speaking to the Council of Europe in May 1978, said:

'In setting up the Commission and the Court, the States for the first time and by virtue of agreements freely entered into submitted themselves to a genuine control mechanism. The right of every citizen of our countries to inform these supervisory organs of the abuses of his own government or of his own bureaucracy confers upon the activity of the Council of Europe the character of a fundamental model. This is truly a decisive turning point in the implementation and the protection of human rights.

'In more than 8000 individual requests the citizens have asked for redress. They have been the object, on the part of the Commission for Human Rights and the Court, of an objective examination of their cause and of mature judgements. Nowhere in the world does there exist such an effective supervision of the internal practices of the States in the matter of human rights. It is equally unique in the sense that human rights are, in the European conception, the true rights of the individual. *We, the European States, consider these rights of the individual as the common juridical patrimony engaging our governmental authority and we therefore submit ourselves to the control of the jurisdiction charged with their application.'*

More recent—created in 1958, it only assumed its full title by the characteristic addition of the second adjective in 1977—the *European Conference of Local and Regional Powers* is still only a technical and purely consultative organ. But it has succeeded in the feat of welcoming to its sessions, at the side of the governmental representatives' delegates sent by the most diverse regional entities from all our countries, Italian regions, Swiss cantons, Länder of the German Federal Republic, even of the transfrontier regions which are taking shape, bridging the frontiers of two and sometimes even three countries. During its annual conventions since 1973, the Conference has brought to light the very original notions of genuine local and regional powers, that is to say authorities endowed with their own finances, legislative councils and executive organs working across the present stato-national frontiers. Lastly, it proposed in 1978—without, however, gaining in the first round the assent of a free and massive majority—the idea of a European Senate of the Regions which seems to be obvious enough to have a good chance of being formed, the only question remaining open being that of the time-lag before this is done.

The European Economic Community

On the side of the Council of Europe, as we have seen, many fertile ideas, many member countries—all those from Western Europe, that is 22 parliamentary democracies out of the 32 or so which exist today in the world—but no powers.

The reverse is true on the side of the European Economic Community of Brussels or the EEC: few new ideas since the founding ideas of Jean Monnet and his team; few Member-States (less than half the European democracies), but some powers over the realities which the majority of Westerners in the twentieth century consider to be the most important: industrial production and trade.

Let us see first what the EEC has produced concretely from 1951 when the Treaty setting up the Coal and Steel Community (ECSC) was signed up to 1979.

To create a *common market* was in the first stage to break down the frontiers which separated the countries of the Community so that men and goods could circulate between Bonn and Paris or between Rome and Copenhagen as easily as between Bordeaux and Marseilles, Naples and Milan; to enable an Italian worker to work without discrimination in Belgium or in Ireland, a Dutch or British consumer to buy Danish or Italian products; to force the French manufacturer to face on equal terms the competition of German or Italian manufacturers.

This 'customs union', with the free circulation of men and goods across the frontiers of the Nine, is what the European Community has achieved since 1968 for the six founder-member countries of the Community and which has been effective since 1977 for all the Nine. The Community is already a single market on which nearly 260 million European consumers can freely draw for supplies.

If customs officers are still encountered at the frontiers between the countries of the Community, this is not because they enforce customs duties which no longer exist: it is because the taxes paid on the sale of goods have not yet been harmonised between the Nine. This harmonisation has been set in train and soon the customs officers will only be there for security reasons and to process statistical statements.

Already these statements reveal that the trade between the countries of the Community has increased by 6% in twenty years. The opportunity to sell on a larger market has given the economy of the Nine an extraordinary boost: in twenty years the income per inhabitant at equal prices has doubled in the Community. (It is true that no one can really be sure what would have happened if the EEC had not existed.)

The creation of a genuine *community,* however, demands more than the setting up of a common market. It necessitates the implementation of policies common to the nine member countries, and this is no easy task.

From the beginning the European Community has possessed a common agricultural policy. It is undoubtedly controversial and must certainly be adjusted. It is blamed for having destroyed the structures of the small and medium enterprises under the pretext of modernisation; of destroying produce in order to maintain the price level in some countries; but it is perhaps thanks to it that the peoples of Europe have for twenty years benefited from abundant agricultural supplies at prices which have given the farmers a decent standard of living.

In the same order of ideas, European industry, with an internal common market of 260 million consumers at its disposal, has been able to rationalise its production. The Community is engaged on a long work of harmonisation of the technical specifications of products which were very different from one country to another and therefore put a brake on the circulation of goods across the frontiers. In order to prevent industrial expansion of the Community from taking place at the expense of the consumers, there is very strict supervision by the European Commission which makes sure that the laws of free competition are rigorously respected. By banning arrangements between industrialists and imposing sometimes very heavy penalties, it conducts a very vigorous 'anti-trust' policy in defence of the consumers.

However, grave difficulties appeared when it came to constructing a genuine industrial policy, especially in the key sectors: in spite of all the efforts, there is still no European policy on information, aeronautics or telecommunications.

Similar difficulties should have been overcome in the realm of scientific and technical research. It is true that research laboratories were set up by the Community in 1960 which employ some 2000 researchers and technicians. But the effort of scientific research continues essentially to take place at the national level.

The research budget of the Community still only absorbs about

1.4% of the total national research budgets of the nine countries.

The Community thus constituted has been able to develop common policy towards the non-Member-States. It speaks with a single voice in international trade negotiations. At the same time it has become the leading trading body in the world.

In this sector this enables the Community to discuss on an equal footing with the greatest—the United States, Canada, Japan, etc.—in order to liberalise international trade.

Its economic expansion confers on the Community special responsibilities with regard to the poorer countries. It gives these a generalised preference for the importation of their products on the communitarian market as well as financial and technical aid of every kind. Most important of all, the Community signed a convention with forty-six emergent countries which was the most generous form of aid ever offered by a group of industrialised countries to a group of developing countries: not only did the European Community freely open its market to most of the products exported by these countries, but it guaranteed them a kind of 'minimal annual guaranteed income' for the sale of their basic products.

It is clear that the commercial weight of the Community on the world scene carries also some political weight. It must, however, be admitted that the Nine, who speak with one voice on commercial affairs, have not the same unanimity when it comes to political matters. And this is explained by the very doctrine on which the European Coal and Steel Community and then the EEC were founded: the idea that the 'factual common interests' and 'common institutions' in the economic sphere would bring about the political unity of the Europeans. 'The Common Market was a means, I would say almost a trick, to build unity on the basis of technique', a former EEC Commissioner stated recently.[1]

But the actions of General de Gaulle in boycotting the EEC for months on end were enough to refute the economist doctrine: political passions were seen to take precedence over economic realities and national prestige over material interests.

The result has been that the economic mechanisms envisaged by Jean Monnet's team, which should have led inevitably to the union of

[1] Jean-Francois Deniau in an interview in l'*Express,* Paris, 10 July 1978.

the Europeans, have been many times diverted, jammed or blocked by the intervention of national sovereignties.

'They were conceived within a very precise political optic, that of the development of a federal Europe [said Jean-Francois Deniau]. Hence the Commission responsible to the Assembly, which is itself elected by European suffrage, hence the vote with qualified majority in the Council. On the American model, the Commission should become the European executive, the elected Assembly the Chamber of Representatives and the Council of Ministers the Senate. The facts have contradicted the dreams.'

In fact the European Council of Heads of State and Prime Ministers, which today represents the supreme organ of the Community, was nowhere foreseen in the Treaty of Rome which set up the Common Market; it is not at all federal, and can only function through unanimity.

The Assembly, elected or not, does not face the Commission, but the Committee of Ministers, that is to say, once again, the Member-States instead of a federal organ.

This is the disappointment of the true pro-Europeans, of the federalists, supporters of a genuine delegation of powers to the various levels of execution, *according to the dimension of the tasks under consideration.*

On an entirely different plane, the deplorable habit must be denounced whereby one speaks currently of the Nine (and yesterday of the Six) as if they were 'Europe', although neither the Scandinavians, nor Switzerland, nor Austria, nor the Iberian countries, nor those of eastern Europe are members of it. This inevitably poses a very important problem: how far can the EEC claim to be the 'kernel of united Europe' so long as no one knows what kind of union it will be: unitary or federalist? Periodically there are proposals made to entrust the EEC with 'enlarged competences', political, social, cultural. It is forgotten that the EEC finding itself thus tempted, not to say constrained, by virtue of its very nature, will apply the criteria of profitability, of productivity or of profit to human activities which arise in reality from very different finalities, qualitative and not quantifiable, affective and spiritual, and not primarily economic.

Cultural and Scientific Activities

As for *cultural activities* in Europe, in the measure in which they influence from near to or distantly the idea of union, it was the *European Cultural Centre* proposed by the Congress in The Hague (1948) that was expressly given the task by the European Conference on Culture, held in Lausanne in 1949. Sponsored from the start by the European Movement, the ECC took the initiative in a certain number of institutions of very varied importance—such as the *European Centre for Nuclear Research* (CERN) in Geneva; the *European Cultural Foundation* in Amsterdam; the *European Association of Music Festivals* (EAMF) in which there are today 38 festivals in 18 countries; the *Association of Institutes of European Studies* (from 34 universities in 10 of our countries); the *European Community of Guilds and Book Clubs,* and the *Campaign for European Civic Education.* But the official sums which are allocated to the ECC—in the order of 0.025% of the cost of building a nuclear plant of 1000 MGW—have rarely enabled it in the European debates to mobilise the wills and to exert sufficient pressure on the national governments. In any case, it is on another plane that one can evaluate the efficiency of organs such as the ECC, the University Institutes of European Studies and the fifty or so periodical publications which they publish; to which must be added the activities of a dozen *Maisons de l'Europe,* of the *European Forum in Alpbach,* which each summer attracts 500 to 600 professors and students to a high valley in the Tyrol, from the *International Centre of European Education* and from the *European Association of Teachers* which each year organise dozens of colloquia in all our countries and, lastly, the research activities of the *European University* which has its seat in Florence.

Present Extent of the European Consensus

It is often said that the idea of European union has not been able to mobilise the masses as they are still mobilised in the Third World by the nationalist idea. And it is true that the crowds do not chant European slogans. But it remains that the idea that union is necessary and possible has found acceptance. It appears that two-thirds of Europeans[1] accept it as a reasonable and accessible objective which no politician dares any longer to contest openly.

This is the result (through repeated polls in the Nine) of long efforts of European information and education undertaken since 1946 by the cultural institutes and the independent researchers who have studied, taught and popularised the principle of the millennial unity of Europe.

A consensus, or in any case a very large majority, of the public opinions in all the countries of the Continent appears very clearly, not only in the public debates but in the subconscious of the great majority of Europeans. It can be described by the factual findings which follow, the importance of which it would be difficult to overestimate.

1. *War between the nations of the new Europe is now unthinkable.* This is not only the result of the treaties nor of the balance of armed forces, but of a profound feeling among the peoples and their intellectual and political élites. A war between France and Germany is no more imaginable today than a war between two Swiss cantons or two American states. The time of the Maginot Line opposing the Siegfried Line is over. This is a radically new element in the political thinking of Europe. The old ideal of a perpetual peace between our nations, which was always treated as ridiculous Utopianism when it was put forward by an Abbot of Saint-Pierre in the eighteenth century, then by a Mazzini or a Victor Hugo in the nineteenth century, is today taken for granted by the vast majority of the European youth.

2. No less fundamental than the definitive rejection of war between our peoples is the necessarily democratic character of the new Europe. To the average European as to our politicians, it goes without saying that a nation dominated by a civil or military dictatorship (Portugal, Spain, Greece only a few years ago) cannot be part of the united or federated Europe. Neither can a nation dominated by a totalitarian party (the countries of eastern Europe, so long as they remain satellites of the USSR). On the other hand, as soon as the Greek, Spanish and Portuguese dictatorships were overthrown, those three countries were

---

[1] For many years public opinion polls in the Nine have invariably shown that 56-66% of the people interrogated are in favour of the idea of the union of Europe. For a more detailed analysis of the attitudes to the election of the European Parliament, see Appendix I.

accepted as candidates for the European Community and integrated
or reintegrated into the Council of Europe.

3. The union of the Europeans must follow the integration of our
national economies. This conviction is today so widespread that to
the immense majority of Europeans, economic integration (partial)
already achieved by the Nine of the Common Market, on the one
hand, and the political union of all Europe which remains to be
brought about, on the other, are very often confused. To most people
the Europe of the Nine is the same as Europe. This is a profound
mistake, as we have seen, but is no less revealing for all that. For if it
is clear that the real Europe cannot be reduced to a common market,
it is no less evident that the economic integration of the Continent
goes beyond and relegates to the past the illusion of 'national economies' those entities which, by some magic, are found to correspond in
the twentieth century to frontiers which have been drawn for centuries
or only for decades through the hazards of wars and treaties.

6. What Has Not Yet Been Done

Such being the evidence and the urgency of the reasons for uniting,
it is surprising that nothing greater or more effective and daring has
been done by our governments to reply to the challenge of the facts.

Neither the European Parliament elected and fully legislative; nor
the Senate of the States or Regions. Nor the Executive under the
command of the Sovereign People represented by these two chambers;
nor a common currency; nor common military defence; nor a common
plan to deal with energy crises such as that of 1973; nor a common
policy against inflation without increasing unemployment and vice
versa.

Nothing far-reaching, effective and daring enough to give credi-
bility in the eyes of our citizens to the Europe of the EEC.

7. What Is Coming

For some years an immense phenomenon has been slowly emerging
in the European consciousness and actuality: this is the germinal
upthrust of European ecological, regionalist, federalist movements,
organically linked in their genesis by a similar reaction against a brutal

world of oppressive uniformity and chalk-line alignments which no longer respect any difference or any minority—neither Nature, nor the regional languages and customs, nor the rights of the individual, which are the foundations of every real community.

A grass-roots movement, spontaneous, pacific and which for the first time for centuries, since the idea of Europe has appeared, enables Europe to look forward to its powerful but non-violent future, to believe in our common future.

This federated Europe of communes, of regions, of nations and of peoples (and no longer of bureaucracies) brings with it its own specific problems: economic, energy, ecological, educational and military. These are what we propose to describe as they are. We, of course, shall not always have solutions to put forward, but we shall try at least to place the problems on their real level.

We are convinced that a united Europe cannot have an answer to everything but that the national sovereignties can no longer supply an answer to anything.

We shall search for some of the main implications of the choices to be made in the face of the structural and organic crisis in the modern world—whether the world is labelled capitalist or socialist, the difference tending to become less and less clear when it comes to the great options of the century such as the material productivity or the quality of life, nuclear energy or solar energy, living equilibrium or equilibrium of terror.

The situation of European union, disappointing at the level of material achievement, nevertheless seems promising when one passes to the political plane, that is to say the moment one passes from the alleged 'necessities' to freely determined objectives.

The pages which follow will sort out the broad lines of a Programme for Europe, dedicated for the first years to the candidates in the election of the century.

1

The Economy

Which Economy?

The general public is too often apt to believe that the economy is an entity with its own laws which it imposes even upon ministers and its own mysteries, impenetrable even to the most learned economists. This superstition is not shared by real economists; its sole beneficiaries are those who know how to force us to accept their proposals as the imperatives of Progress and their desires as our fatalities. For all the rest, it is generally admitted that 'the laws of economic Progress' cause as much stress as they bring well-being, even a little more and very much more in times of crisis.

Now crisis has become the rule (if not the norm) in all the Western economies and the ever-darkening horizon of Progress according to the creed of the European nineteenth century adopted by the vast masses of the twentieth.

In this sphere there are no laws or mysteries except those of the man who has made the economy and because of whom alone it is in crisis. In the world which surrounds us, where everything is the work of man, even the countryside and the deserts (above all, the latter), the economy, like science, in the last analysis can only study the projection of our needs or rather of our desires, true or false, provoked by advertising, fashion and the imitation of our neighbour. Everything comes back to the options and the desires of man.

Hence it follows that to change our desires—to change our hearts, as we used to say—is the only realistic solution for our so-called economic crisis.

It would be well to remember these remarks when reading what follows.

1. The Economic State of Europe

Growth but Dissatisfaction

The Community in Brussels seems in twenty-five years to have achieved most of its immediate economic objectives. The liberalisation of trade achieved in 1977 made possible the creation of a vast market and mass production. By the game of expansion and concentrations, the industry of the Six, then of the Nine, has been able to approach the levels of the great American industry. For the Community, 'Europe' is already a reality.

As for the population of our countries: governmental or private reports describing the state of Western society constantly boast of the 'extraordinary improvement in the material well-being of the Europeans' and give as an example the improvement in their *food,* their *habitat,* their *conditions of work,* the *opportunities for education* and *health* which are offered to them as well as the *increased leisure* and, finally, their *prolonged life expectation.*

But in fact most Europeans feel strongly—and innumerable scientific studies have shown this—that it is too often the reverse which is true and which we daily experience:

— our *food,* in general too copious, is more and more denaturalised; products of conservation, colouring agents and refinements (often cancer-inducing), chemical oils, pesticides, hormones; adulterated wines, polluted waters recycled six to eight times, etc.;

— the urban *habitat* is becoming more expensive, more asocial or anti-social, more anonymous, more wasteful of energy, noisier and far less safe;

— the *conditions of work* have deteriorated in many industries: accidents, contamination, accelerated rhythms, intolerable shifts;

— the lengthening of the commuting time taken between one's home and place of work reduces the time left for leisure (the French expression *metro-boulot-dodo*[1] expresses it very well);

— the *opportunities for education,* theoretically broader, are in

---

[1] Tube-work-bed.

fact restricted by the constantly increasing demands for speciali-
sation and by the standardising grip of the, to all intents, State-
owned TV channels which are rightly called 'chains' in French
and which propagate and import stereotypes, clichés, fashions
and prejudices at the expense of the critical spirit;

— lastly, the *prolonged life expectation* is also called the aging of
the population and is one of the most alarming and difficult
problems facing our industrial society.

Most of our contemporaries seem to be unaware of these facts,
masked by advertising and a deliberate policy of reflating the economy
so that not one of our governments dares to reconsider it although
they are aware that they are simply delaying the day of reckoning until
the opposition is returned to power.

The dissatisfaction is not the result of material growth in itself but
rather springs from the fact that the people have been persuaded that
this growth could bring them a well-being proportionate to the rate of
growth of the GNP. The reverse is what is happening.

One fine day, when one hears over the State radio that tobacco is
the cause of more deaths in one country of the EEC than the motor-
car and that although the taxes on tobacco bring to the State so many
millions per year, the costs of hospitalisation, insurance and other
expenses incurred for those who are ill because they smoke have almost
doubled, one forgets to draw the conclusion that the worse things
become in that sector (for the health and for the pocket of the taxpayer) the more the GNP increases and allows the prime minister to
speak of 'the constantly improving health of the economy of our
country'. In other terms, the health of the economy is sometimes
the reverse of that of the citizens.

It must be added that the introduction of systems of industrialisation
into the social structures of the Third World, which is not ready to
receive them, has destroyed even more than in Europe the inestimable
benefits and values of daily use, with the result that industrialisation
has produced just as much poverty for a great number as it has riches
for a small number. It has greatly reinforced the inequalities between
the classes, between the countries, between the north and the south.

All Rapid Progress Creates New and Unexpected Problems

Notwithstanding these disappointments, the 'public', that is the opinion created by advertising and industry, have been in agreement, during the last thirty years, to develop the kind of society which is most favourable to the maximisation of production and of living standards, that is, of consumption.

But simply because of this 'progress' or rather of this progression and of its rapidity, some new problems have arisen:

(a) Institutions are slow to adapt: *economic legislation is no longer able to protect quickly enough the consumer and the saver;* municipalities are no longer able to prevent a chaotic urbanisation; the public services (transport, post, telegraph and telephone) are overwhelmed; hospitals, universities, social services are in a state of permanent crisis—under-financed, over-worked and with too many calls upon them.

(b) *Delinquency* and crime increase in the urban centres, individual and collective violence becoming a reflex to resolve the anguishing difficulties of a too rapidly changing world; dishonesty increases in protest against bureaucracy.

(c) *Collective convictions,* religious or ideological, are weakening and little by little are losing their power to cope with material problems, which are multiplied rather than resolved by the industrial civilisation.

(d) Far from diminishing, *social discriminations* are becoming sharper and the antipathy against marginal or minority groups, such as immigrant workers or militant workers, is becoming more widespread among the population.

(e) *The aberrant vulnerability of the Western economy as a whole* was seen in the autumn of 1973: it would only need an embargo (by the USSR perhaps) on the oil of the Gulf States for everything to grind to a halt.

(f) This gives the Europeans *a growing sense of insecurity.* The individual no longer feels that he is a part of a protective social structure, as was the family, but feels that he is delivered defenceless to the collective pressures of the modern world. Outside his hours of work (most often tedious) and his hours of travel (most often irritating) his leisure time is broken in upon by other social pressures (TV, advertising) which push him towards ever-greater consumption, expense, the need to earn more and therefore to frustration and insecurity.

(g) Born of a feeling of insecurity, or of the inability to understand what is happening, this insecurity generates an anxious nervousness in which can be found one of the causes of the *present inflationary pressures*. This is what motivates the trade unions in their demands for higher wages. This explains why the consumers, the victims of multiple pressures, the nature of which they do not understand, accept the arbitrary price increases. Lastly, it explains why the governments think it necessary to increase still more expansion in order to obtain in the near future what has not been obtainable in the present.

The question which must be answered is that of whether the present crisis is merely an accident in the general development of the world towards productivity and increased consumption or an alarm signal warning of the urgent need for a very different development, for a genuine change of direction.

2. The Crisis

Unanswered Questions Proliferate

Seen in a worldwide perspective, Europe was not only the initiator of the industrial adventure but its first testing ground.

Lacking raw materials, Europe was condemned to manufacturing techniques. Its fate was to become the most intense centre of productivity and of world expansion: this was the history of the nineteenth century and of colonisation. Colonisation received its greatest impetus during the 1880s and came to an end to all intents in 1934 with the invasion of Abyssinia. The decolonisation which followed the Second World War had finished by the 1960s as regards to Great Britain, France, Holland and Belgium. Portugal was to follow a little later: Mozambique, Angola, 1975-6.

Having discovered the whole world, at a time when no one had succeeded in discovering it, Europe, greedy for new things, curious about everything, missionising not only of its dominant religion which it claimed was universal (Catholic) but of the ideologies which stemmed from it through secularisation (such as democracy, socialism, the rights of man) or by the rejection of its fundamental spiritual and universal beliefs (hence the capitalist or Marxist materialism and the ever-growing totalitarian nationalisms), naturally was the first to reach the stage of questioning the ideas which governed 'industrial progress', that is to say of the belief in human Progress obtained through the multiplication of goods and the increase in the GNP.

The portents had appeared long before, but it was clearly the events of 1973-5 which *declared the crisis* and which shattered the general confidence in the unlimited rapid unproblematic growth of our economies.

The present crisis, which goes beyond the field of the economy, results at once in a conjectural recession, structural flaws in the model of growth which are everywhere accepted, and in the emerging awareness that a change is necessary in the choice of the finalities of our existence on earth and the priorities which result from these choices.

Have we the right to burn all the oil of the earth, leaving to our descendants only the administration of enormous radioactive stocks to cool for 120,000 years or else blow everything up? Is it progress to increase our needs? Progress towards what? Is it a reasonable wager or a rush towards the collective suicide of the species?

One question runs like a network of filagree through these doubts: 'When we have gained the world at the price of our souls, what will remain for us to love?'

Many Causes, Similar Effects

Economic in the strictest sense, the present crisis has many causes such as the *demographic explosion,* the monetary *anarchy* and *speculation,* the rise in the *price of oil,*[1] the threat posed by *shortages of energy* and the *exhaustion of non-renewable resources,* the alarming increase in pollution from industrial activities, the unscrupulous appli-

---

[1] The price of oil has multiplied by five between 1972 and 1979. This already inconveniences motorists but not governments which raise from 55% to 66% the 'fiscal' taxes on the price of petrol and have an interest in the increase in the basic prices they pay in devalued dollars. European public opinion appears not to worry about this. To attempt to understand these matters might take you too far.

cation of all the technical inventions which can increase the *competitiveness* of an enterprise or of a State despite every other 'reason' and of any possible consequences which may be damaging for Nature and for mankind.

But the crisis has similar effects, such as the aberrant *vulnerability* of economic systems, proportional to their centralisation and their gigantism, *inflation, unemployment* and the *deterioration of human relations* which result from it.

Inflation and Unemployment

According to the monetarists we have consulted, the *inflation* which characterises the Western economy was caused first of all by the Vietnam War, the effects of which were exported to Europe. This war once ended, its consequences were prolonged and enlarged. But it is clear that this conjunctural motive, which today has disappeared, is added to general motives such as the popular belief—both capitalist and Marxist—that material growth is synonymous with better living and the passive acceptance of the 'savage' implementation of new techniques, provided that they are put forward as profitable in the short term.

From the Utopia of permanent and infinite material growth—clearly impossible in a finite world—and of the dictatorship of 'technological imperatives', there result inflation and unemployment, those two complementary or collusive illnesses.

The size of the rate of growth of inflation in the countries of the EEC is known: from 7% to 8% per year, on average, with rises for some of 13.7%, even 15.9%, and a minimum of 3.1% or even 2.1% for others.

As for unemployment, two figures will suffice here: 6.1 million demands for jobs unsatisfied in the Nine at the end of 1978 compared with 2.65 in 1974.[1]

The present unemployment is clearly due in part to automation, that is to industrial 'progress' which substitutes the machine for the worker; in part to the huge investments in the energy sector, in which capital counts far more than work; in part to the transfer (by the

[1] On the present state of inflation and of unemployment in the Europe of the Nine, see Appendix II.

multinationals) of our technologies to the Third World; lastly to a certain fatigue in the consumer society.

Unemployment is therefore not a conjunctural accident in our society. It arises from the very structures of this society and from its sacrosanct principles of the priority of profit and of endless productivity gained by technologies.

Examples:

— the new techniques in steel, applied by Japan, will enable a reduction of 70% of jobs in this branch to be made (and already the European steel production is in a grave crisis);

— from 1952 to 1973 the number of technicians employed in the petro-chemical industry in France has increased by 150% but that of the workers has diminished from 28% to 6%;

— the new machines used for the felling or mechanical plantation of forests has made it possible in ten years to get rid of two-thirds of the forestry workers;

— in France alone, in the Post Office, 150,000 jobs have been put in jeopardy by the technical invention called Visual Display Unit (VDU) by which letters can be sent by TV from one house to another in 30 seconds;

— each new nuclear power plant producing 1000 MGW will make possible the suppression, through automation, of a minimum of 4000 jobs;

— competition in the motor-car industry will compel the Europeans to halve the number of workers employed in this branch.

The cumulative effects of inflation and of unemployment have an inevitably *damaging effect on the social climate.* In the majority of our countries—above all in the larger ones—we see a polarisation of public opinion which creates inexpiable hatreds between Right and Left which are more symbolic and mythical than real, but which relentlessly result in the wholesale and final condemnation of one half of a country by the other, and, vice versa, in the name of principles and ends between which it is becoming more and more difficult to distinguish and, *a fortiori,* to oppose on the great themes of *growth at any price,* of *nuclear armaments,* of *atomic energy* and of the exploitation of the Third World under the name of co-operation: hard-line communists and conservatives vote together on all these choices—which are the fundamental choices of the century.

In this way the conviction spreads that the Western-type economy can no longer be mastered, either by the Right which created it or by the Left which fears rather than desires to inherit it. 'At the end of the present economic policy there is nothing except an aggravation of one or other of the aspects of the crisis: at the end of periods of control there is more unemployment, at the end of periods of expansion, there is more inflation.'[1]

After an exceptionally 'favourable' period of the exploitation of the technology based on science, one can see that this same technology is no longer able to develop at the speed and in the conditions necessary in order that economic growth should produce genuine 'well-being'. The law of diminishing returns of technology, as it appears, will dominate from now on the relation between industrial progress and human well-being.

In the industrial countries increasingly strong social pressure impatient to change substantially the distribution of wealth in favour of labour has reinforced the demand for collective equipment. From these accumulated pressures on the economic systems a new form of generalised inflation has resulted and a reduction in investments which to all intents has put an end to the 'exponential' dynamism of growth.

Inflation, unemployment, recession, growing instability of the international monetary system are thus aspects of one and the same structural crisis.

And we see that our States have not got the means to master them on the national scale. Neither can the political parties show us convincingly how to break out of the vicious circle of the crisis in the productivist system within which they confront one another.

A last word: the worst danger which threatens Europe—and rightly itself first, but with it tomorrow the Third World—is not the industrial recession nor the exhaustion of resources nor the high taxes nor inflation nor even the rise in unemployment. The worst danger lies in an economic policy which tries to break out of these dead ends by exporting to the Third World the very causes of our own crisis and

[1] J. Attali, *Le Monde,* 14 April 1977. (Mr. Attali is economic adviser to Francois Mitterrand, the leader of the French Socialist Party.)

the means—especially nuclear—to put an end to it either by the enslave-ment of its fomenters or by the destruction of its victims who find that they are the same, that is ourselves.

It is our model of growth which must be changed, our ideology of growth and the national frameworks in which we want to measure its 'progress'.

3. Solutions Possible Through Union and By a Concomitant Restructuring

> Economic knowledge should be established not on the premises of the will for power and the profit motive, but on those of good organisation of human groups according to the very etymology of the expression.
>
> *Albert Tévoédjrè, La Pauvreté, richesse des peuples*

> Unidimensional economic growth ends in an increase in wants, not in happiness.
>
> *Indira Gandhi*

All this leads us to the conclusion that there are no purely economic solutions for the present economic crisis.

Governments announce every six months measures designed to bring us out of the tunnel of inflation or unemployment. However, neither the capitalist nor the social democratic nor the communist States can boast that they have found the best solutions for these prob-lems: they have tackled them in fact in the name of these same prin-ciples of unrestricted growth and in the same national framework in which these problems show that they are insoluble by definition.

All the recent research in the United States and in Europe on 'the quality of life' agrees that this is not a 'national' problem: the quality of life depends on the individual's perception of the state of the econo-mic, social and political system in which he lives. Now this percep-tion is directed first towards the restricted geographical milieu in which he leads his daily life: his habitat, his place of work, the means of transport and the collective services which he uses, the local or regional institutions in which he can take part. *A policy of 'quality of life' is in fact a policy which decentralises to the maximum the real powers and encourages the direct participation of the citizens on the most immediate levels of decision-making, closest to the life of the community.*

From the industrial era we must pass to the era of human resources.

The industrial era, because it sought the maximisation of production, no matter what the social cost might be, called for the concentration of efforts—centralism. It demanded both a national planning and beyond that larger markets like 'the Europe of the Six', then of the Nine or Twelve. The progress of the multinational was written into this so-called economic 'necessity'.

The era of human resources, on the contrary, because it puts well-being first, calls for decentralisation, local initiative, autonomy, a remodelling of the methods of mass production and regional planning.

Of the processes of solidarity. Nevertheless, not all economic activities can be decentralised. Arbitration remains desirable or necessary at the supraregional or national, as well as world or continental level; the process of solidarity remains to be established or maintained, for the inequalities in the distribution of wealth among the regions, accentuated today by the very process of industrial growth must be attenuated if not completely corrected.

It is then that Europe—but in the broad sense of the union of all its countries—will rediscover a meaning in the organised momentum of transnational solidarities.

Need for a new European model. Europe today needs a true regional plan which will transcend the political and customs barriers and give the world a great example of the ability of our peoples to solve a problem which is crucial for the future of the whole of mankind; that of the fulfilment of our hopes in terms both of the standard and the quality of life and in full solidarity with the inhabitants of other continents.

The lack, up to now, of such a programme explains the crisis in the European movement. To the external observer what is most lacking in the present Europe are true forecasts of the future which could give again a European motivation to the general public in our countries.

Possible programmes, motivating possibilities. Hitherto one could say, although it is a simplification, that the attempts to draw up European programmes have resulted in failure. It is not the few technological achievements or their industrial impact (in the realm of space, or aerospace), and still less the 'common agricultural market', which can really motivate the future shaping of Europe. However, it is not that we have lacked opportunities: it is the global design, the project of a society which goes beyond the industrial era in that it tries no longer to subordinate the economy to profit but to man.

The present energy crisis offers us the opportunity to create a European programme which will not only enable us in the long run to escape from our present dependence on the Arabs to a dependence on the Americans, the Russians and the African dictatorships, but which will, above all, enable us to reach a system of energy supply which will be integrated within the other economic, social and cultural activities of our regions. And this programme, which will include the fundamental research of *all* the sources of energy (particularly that of solar energy) could give to Europe once again its pioneering aspect in a domain which is today decisive for the long-term survival of mankind.

A European project in the realm of *transport* could rest on the need for rapid railway links between the great urban decision-making centres and the generalised substitution of public transport for private cars which would be both an economy (time, petrol, costs, efficiency) and beneficial for the morale of the users.

A food programme should rely upon the existence of a decentralised industry in this sector, supported by a global policy.

A commercial programme could prevent the result that the sale to the countries of the Third World of ready-made factories should lead both to unemployment and the growth of our imports.

Two immediate consequences can be drawn from this:

(1) No European economy without a European policy. While we are witnessing a globalisation of the problems on a world scale, which is increased by interdependence and which jeopardises the future of mankind, the world needs a strong and united Europe able to carry out an important task at the level of the solidarity of all the peoples on earth.

(2) No true 'European Community' without participation at all levels of decision making.

In the industrial society devoted to quantitative production and consumption, according to the inexplicable calculations of distant and anonymous centres, the individual no longer feels that he is protected by customary and stable social structures. Without any guarantee for his daily work, without any power over the economic and monetary policies which decide his fate, he is delivered, defenceless, to the massive external pressures of the State, of the market, of employers or of an advertising climate which drags him into the obsessive pursuit of material 'satisfactions' which are very seldom attainable or seldom satisfying if by any chance they are attained.

Hence the feeling of insecurity and of frustration which is characteristic of our social climate and which reveals the disastrous decadence of the communitarian realities in the West.

One of the reasons for this is the growing distance between the individual and the decision-making processes which affect his present and his future: he no longer has any power over them.

In political terms, the remedy should therefore lie in the *renewal of interest in local and regional communities:* there alone men and women can make their voices heard, can be free because they are responsible.

The remedies for the economic crisis lie in a new method of analysing human needs, starting with the organically and morally vital needs and not from the sole profit motive of the great enterprises. Hence, the creation of small units of production, bringing about a more genuine participation in decisions; and certainly a new evaluation of the role of governments—instruments in the service of the citizens.

Activities, Employment, Unemployment

It has been calculated that all the tasks of an industrial State, including the agencies for unemployment and the other social services, could be carried out by 15% of the labour force available. This change, although difficult, is not impossible. It would demand long-term and probably unpopular policies at the beginning in some countries but it could lead to a type of society which would maintain a high material standard of living and at the same time create opportunities for education and culture which today are inconceivable.

The number of unemployed in the world increases by 100 per minute.[1] In this situation it is no longer a question of 'stimulating demand' (artificially) or of seeking the dilution of the labour force by the introduction of unnecessary jobs and lower productivity.

[1] Report published on 22 August 1978 in Geneva by the International Labour Office (U.N.O.).

A consensus is being formed and is beginning to appear among the most serious economists (that is, the least routine-like) in the Third World, as in the United States and Europe as well as among the non-communist trade unions. The solutions to the crucial problem of unemployment as a structural product of the industrial society must be found at once in the following directions:

— to shorten the hours of work;

— to prolong (genuinely, that is, having deducted the time taken by commuting) the time of leisure or the time free for other activities;

— to develop a more autonomous agriculture better suited to the specific conditions—ecological and social—of the European regions; more diversified; importing less energy; more concerned about qualitative results than quick profits gained at the expense of the systems and the regimes of social, psychological and cultural relations of a given population in Europe as well as in the Third World;

— to develop a communitarian class of craftsmen, family-based or individual, and all forms of manual crafts; to increase alternative employment (not concerned with the age limit);

— to reduce the bureaucracy by an effective decentralisation, up to regional level, which would allow the regions to take the initiative again (within the general framework and leading to the eventual conciliation of agencies of national or federal concertations);

— to regionalise the adjustments of the supply and demand of jobs, modulate the orientation towards diversified jobs according to the customs and relations of the neighbourhood, taking advantage of the more obvious and multiple local opportunities to combine the activities of different sectors;

— to obtain an international concertation of the transfer of technologies in order to prevent the destruction of the ecosystems in the recipient countries so that they do not increase unemployment in the country of origin—the latter becoming the importer of products of his own technique to the detriment of his own enterprises which are bankrupted and dismiss their work force.

All the signposts point to a similar concern to put order into the economy—the work of men and the means of subsistence which they draw from it for the real well-being of the greatest possible number of real people rather than for the cash profit of an ever-smaller number of companies ever more anonymous and ever more irresponsible.

Urgency

It is time to set the economy to work for the recognised aims of our society and no longer for the pretended 'imperatives' which prevent us from doing so 'for the moment'.

It is time to look for the immediate means to obey a single unquestionable imperative: that of nuclear disarmament, the condition for the survival of the human race as a civilisation.

It is time to liberate the world economy from its most anguishing servitude: the production at a cost of 350 milliard dollars per year of armaments whose only use is to neutralise each other potentially and which are, at best, of no use.

And it is time to put this economy, freed from its obsession with war, that is with the suicide of the species, to work for humane ends which are also at the limits set by the social and natural realities which it thought it had banished from its accounts.

It is high time that R&D (the Research and Development initials and expressions made sacred by contemporary industry and technocracy) should be turned towards *new realms* as yet uncolonised by the Nation-States, as yet unstructured and dimensioned by the 'imperatives' of preparation for war, and thus of centralisation.

Speaking of the setting up of federal structures in Europe, Louis Armand formulated a golden rule which is applicable here: 'Let us develop in common what is new. Let us leave aside the legacies from the past which it would take too long to unify, would demand too much energy and arouse too much opposition.'

If we really want to unite Europe we must find a starting point other than the divisive factors; we must build on something other than on the obstacles to union, hope on a plane other than the one on which union has been shown to be impossible. We shall find these new or evolving realities which are now in the process of full transformation in the sphere of Energy, in the problems of the Ecology, and in the rise of the Regions.

2

Energy

1. The Energy Situation

A few figures and a few dates will be sufficient to describe the *global* problem of energy:

World Consumption of Energy

in 1900   500 million MTOE (million tonnes of oil equivalent)
in 1950   1700 million MTOE (million tonnes of oil equivalent)
in 1974   5800 million MTOE (million tonnes of oil equivalent)
in 2000 (forecast) 15-18 milliard MTOE[1]

For the Europe of the Nine, the energy balance will be established as follows:

	In 1973 (million MTOE)	In 1985 (estimation) (million MTOE)
Production (including nuclear)	370	640
Imports	635	1160
Consumption	1005	1800

The global consumption of energy, according to most of the forecasts presented to the World Energy Conference held in Istanbul in October 1977, should increase continuously until 2020 when it will reach a total of 44 milliard MTOE.[2]

But according to the same official experts the world production of energy in 2020 can in no case reach more than 25 milliard MTOE. A shortfall of 19 milliard MTOE must be foreseen.

[1] Source: WAES Reports, *Energy Global Prospects 1985-2000,* New York, 1977.
[2] Statement of John Hill, President of the British Atomic Energy Authority, in Istanbul.

It is in this global perspective that the figures for the Nine must be read. These countries, taken separately, have very unequal resources. Great Britain has coal, oil, natural gas and nuclear energy; Italy has hydroelectric power and natural gas; Holland has a lot of natural gas but no coal and no hydraulic or nuclear energy; France has no longer much coal or gas, but a powerful hydraulic capacity and a most ambitious nuclear programme; so has the German Federal Republic which also has a lot of lignite and coal. It can be deduced from this that a common policy is called for in the energy sector more than in any other. Each of our countries is constrained to face up to the same problem of general immediate policy: that of the dependence of these countries for oil on OPEC and/or the United States, on Canada, Black Africa, then later South Africa for uranium, and on the USSR for enriched uranium.

This dependence can only increase with the increase in the consumption of energy until the time comes—in twenty or thirty years—in which the relative shortage of primary energy (oil, then uranium) on the world scale will become for the Europeans an *absolute* economic disaster if the 'economic logic' remains what it is today.

Criticism of the Basic Assumptions of the Problem

But is this increase in consumption fatal? Can the postulate, on which all the quoted forecasts rest according to which economic growth, energy growth and well-being are inseparable, not be contested? Lastly, is it excluded that the demand in energy should adapt itself to the decreasing supply?

The studies of perspectives undertaken in the United States, Canada, Great Britain and France show that a state of *shortage,* that is of the exhaustion of exploitable reserves in the time-limits and at supportable costs, will make itself felt:

— for *oil* in 1985 or 1995 or 2000 at the latest (according to the scenarios drawn up by the different research groups);
— for *natural gas* from 1985 onwards;
— for *uranium* from 1990.

It must be repeated that all these forecasts presuppose continued (even although slowed up) growth in the consumption of energy; *but is this how the problem should be put?*

What could be, in fact, the reasons for increasing our consumption of energy seeing that:

— the demographic growth of the Europeans tends towards zero in several countries and is already negative in some, including the German Federal Republic;
— unemployment continues to rage (see above for the structural reasons);
— production has everywhere slowed down (the OECD forecast in 1974 a growth of 5.1% but it has reduced its rate to 4% in 1976, to 3.5% in 1978: some countries are at 2%);
— excessive consumption is everywhere denounced and recognised, the fight against waste is entrusted to *ad hoc* ministerial departments?

On examination, the reasons claimed as obvious and put forward in support of the unrelenting increase in our energy consumption are revealed as bad ones, not only as debatable but reversible.

There is, first, the enormous propaganda for waste: producers of electricity, motor-car manufacturers, and builders of motor-ways, skyscrapers and nuclear plants speak only of the 'growing need' for what they produce. But once again it is clear that they *are trying to make us take their desires for our fatalities.*

Then there is the advertisement for the 'all electric':[1] an avowed method for making nuclear power plants appear 'necessary', 'the only substitutes for foreign oil'.[2] There are, lastly, the bad habits adopted by the private or public users of electricity or of petrol; the construction of maximum energy-devouring 'towers'; the bad insulation of buildings; too fierce central heating and air-conditioning, these two excesses added together far from neutralise each other; advertisements

---

[1] Heating by electricity with its yield of 6%, which is the worst in the world, has been rightly called 'the energy crime'.

[2] Cf. the interview of the General Director of L'Electricité de France (EDF) published by *Le Monde,* 24 January 1975.

in neon lights; the contracts which favour the greatest consumers of kilowatts.

In fact it has never been proved that the demand for energy must continue to increase indefinitely without adapting itself to the eventually failing supply. What is certain, on the other hand, is that the realisable savings in energy in the near future already constitute for Europe its main source of autonomous energy. Many scientists have estimated at 20%, even 30%, the possible savings in present consumption without any diminution in production or comfort, while nuclear energy at best can only supply 17% of the total consumption in 1985 and, much more probably, 9% (forecast of the EEC).

2. The Alternative Solutions

The governments of the Nine and the Commission itself state that the only alternative to oil twenty or thirty years from now will be nuclear energy. Three remarks on this:

(a) Just when the oil fails[1] the shortage of uranium will appear. The alternative to the present power plants will be the fast breeder reactors.

But it is neither certain nor probable that the fast breeder reactors planned in France, in Great Britain and in the German Federal Republic can be built. Let us mention the main obstacles which are already known:

— the resistance of the people, the visceral fear of the nuclear, the 'trauma of Hiroshima' which is an important fact in spite of what the technocrats may say who themselves have felt nothing and fear nothing if they are to be believed;
— the negative votes of several general and regional councils in France, in the Swiss cantons and communes, in the Länder of the GFR, in the whole of Austria at the end of 1978.

---

[1] It will be perhaps 50 or 100 years later than the forecasters foresaw. It seems that Mexico can produce as many millions of barrels of oil as all the other parts of the world together. Let us note that those who cast doubt on these facts are precisely the promoters of nuclear energy.

— the determined and documented opposition of thousands of scientists in all our countries;[1]
— the opposition of all the ecological associations and of their hundreds of thousands of militants;
— the grave technical doubts as to the security of the apparatuses built, already twice found faulty at Creys-Malville;
— the raw materials required (uranium and thorium) which will be exhausted at the same time as oil;
— the dependence on foreign co-operation (techniques, licences, stocks of uranium, recycling, plants for storing the radioactive waste, financing);
— the astronomical costs, which continue to increase, of the nuclear power plants, which demand investments out of all proportion to the short period during which they can be used, and to the period of 24,000 to 120,000 years during which they will impose daily and continuous charges on future generations;
— the indispensable international financing, in flagrant contradiction to the official declarations on 'the national independence', which will be guaranteed by nuclear power;[2]
— the real price of nuclear energy, far higher than the prices announced because of the always hidden costs of dismantling the plants after thirty years and the management of radioactive waste and explosive for 120,000 years;
— lastly—and this is perhaps the most effective argument—contrary to all the official propaganda, unemployment is increased by the nuclear power plants. Each of them, enabling the improvement of the automisation of industrial prospection, at the same time enables 4000 jobs to be suppressed.[3]

[1] See in particular the manifestoes published by the members of the Collège de France in Paris; of CERN in Geneva; of the whole of France: 400, 1200, 4000 signatures.
[2] See *Le Rapport de la Commission des Finances du Parlement francais,* September 1977, N° 3131, which decisively eliminates this argument.
[3] The Swiss passed a law in 1959 which was very favourable to nuclear power plants. One of the main arguments in the campaign was that nuclear plants would *do away with tens of thousands of jobs* by increasing automation. (There was a shortage of man-power at the time.) Ten years later the reverse was argued, cynically: to stop building the plants would be to create unemployment, we were told. Who dares to take the responsibility, repeat some newspapers and those who finance them.

(b) There exist in fact many other possibilities for remedying the shortage of oil and of uranium, other known sources of energy; above all, solar, then geothermal, from wind, biological, hitherto underestimated by the officially sponsored research and by the EEC itself, whose budget for 1978 allocated 66 million units of account for the nuclear against 6 million for all the 'other forms' of energy. To which must be added the cycle of oxides of carbon for the plastics and carburant industries, and, lastly, coal which is still very abundant in Europe.

(c) The EEC has launched a very far-reaching research project devoted to nuclear fusion, a process reputedly 'clean' and not creating wastes other than H_2O—water. If ever this form of energy were to become industrial, which is in itself very far from certain, it will nevertheless have two grave drawbacks:

(1) It will seem to absolve those who have the responsibility from asking themselves the primordial question of how much energy is necessary for the happiness of mankind, that is for their equilibrium in the town and with nature;

(2) it will create a physical, financial and administrative centralisation of the sources of energy which will make them more vulnerable to air attack or to commando raids.

Instead of hypnotising ourselves with the indefinite growth of the consumption of energy, which can only lead to dramatic impasses; instead of accepting uncritically the dogma of the parallelism between the growth of energy, economic growth and well-being, which each day shows anew that it is less credible, it is time to envisage a change of course and to review the whole European energy policy—or, to put it better: to create one which is worthy of the name, taking into consideration the goals of civilisation which would not be solely profit in money, military power in nuclear weapons and the raising, regardless of the cost, of the material standard of living at the expense of Nature, of well-being, of liberties and of the meaning of life.

3. Solutions on the Continental Scale

(1) In the event of a new oil crisis (war in the Middle East) to foresee measures of European solidarity which will exclude the painful

situation of 1973 in which we saw one of the Six being discriminated against, others paying court to the producing countries, etc.

(2) To be aware that nuclear energy (practically the fast breeder reactors from 1990) can only be set up under the protection of the police, even of the army[1] and of a new ideological inquisition, which means it will be at the expense of human rights and of democratic liberties. While, on the other hand, solar energy, *which is everywhere,* calls for and permits decentralised regimes and local autonomies, i.e. the very conditions of peace.

(3) To pursue the research for non-nuclear forms of energy, hitherto marginalised by our States, all centralisers and thus obsessed with the idea of 'great plants'. To this end, to pool brains and investments, as was done for CERN and more recently for the study of nuclear biology, and of thermonuclear fusion; and that, beyond the Nine, that is to say for *all* the countries which recognise that they are Europeans in the East as in the West.

(4) To guarantee to the populations concerned on the local and regional levels the right to vote on the setting up of energy-producing works.

(5) To draw up a common policy of transport in the towns and countryside.

(6) To put in hand urgently the study—in a European pool—of the post-petroleum society: what should be done, what society should we foresee once we are deprived of oil? How can we prepare now for the transition to such a society? What are the technological requirements?

(7) To diminish (by communitarian decisions) the rate of growth of energy consumption (the Carter plan forecasts a fall from 5% to 2%), the consumption of petrol by motor-cars (Carter plan: less 10%), the temperature maximum of buildings heated by crude oil.

(8) It has been proposed to reduce by 15% through the voluntary decision of the citizens the private consumption of energy by instituting one day and night per week a day of wood fires and candles. This is

---

[1] 'It is essential that the nuclear power plants which will be built be fewer, thus of big size, implanted on *ad hoc* sites and *run on quasi-military lines:* statement by M. Jean-Claude Leny, General Director of FRAMATOME, the company in France which constructs PWR plants under the Westinghouse licence (*Investir,* 24 March 1975).

reasonable and full of charm, but not enough. It would be preferable, for example, to eliminate by European agreement electric heating and generally the processes of notoriously insufficient yield.

(9) If our States insist on making propaganda, let it be for the increasingly frequent and ingenuous utilisation of *human energy*— what the motor-car and a hundred forms of waste incite us to neglect, to overlook and to condemn.

These measures, among so many others, already put forward or still to be conceived by the competent scientists, all presuppose either a consensus of the ministers of the European Community which should be signed at once by the non-member European States; or the setting up of a European Energy Council formed by delegates from the twenty-two Western countries until those of eastern Europe can join it should they want to. There is only one solution to the energy problem: the United Europe.

3

Environment

1. The Ecological Concern

Reaction to the Industrial Aggression

The ecology with which we are dealing is a policy of life and of the dynamic balance in the living world in so far as it is threatened by the encroaching industrial civilisation. Ecology reminds us that technical progress and science itself can do nothing against the fundamental laws of Nature, and if we try to ignore these laws we put the survival of mankind in jeopardy.

The ecology is therefore a true policy not in the sense of partisan rivalries but in that of the strategies of a civilisation. As the forecast of the health and creative activity of our Western society, it is therefore policy *par excellence* if it is still true that 'to govern is to foresee'.

The ecological concern often irresponsibly described as a 'fashion' is really a reaction against the 'fashion' of concreting the countryside, of the industrial pollution of the air, of the soil, of the waters and of the oceans by the production, the transportation and the wasteful use of primary sources of energy.

The ecological concern responds to the extinction of hundreds of animal species (whales, elephants, seals, butterflies), to the accumulation of radioactive waste which no one knows how to get rid of and 'which must be completely isolated in the biosphere for 200,000 to 240,000 years, a far longer period than that of the history of mankind'.[1]

The ecological concern is caused also by the shortages which will appear at the end of this century: shortages of petrol, uranium, drinking water and possibly of oxygen, if we continue to destroy the main

[1] *State of the Environment, 1975, Programme of the United Nations for the Environment,* p. 12.

sources of production: the plankton in the oceans and the forests, 40% of which have already been destroyed in the world since 1882.

The relation between the ecology and the many varied forms of aggression by the industrial technostructure against Nature, against the communities, against the physiology of the species and the individual, are similar to the relation between medicine and the 'ills of civilisation' such as cancer and coronaries.

It is mainly through fear of the possible effects of nuclear energy—bombs or power plants—on the natural or urban environment, that this ecological concern has been awakened in the youth and among the intellectuals and scientists in our countries in so far as they feel themselves to be and want to be responsible towards society.

The resistance to nuclear power arises from such commonsense questions as: Why do we need so much (and always more) energy? Can we not reach our goals at less expense? Or use more efficiently what we have?[1] To which can be added: What price have we paid for this surplus of energy? and more generally: What price have we paid for material Progress? The price being perhaps that of our vital environment—of our survival.

Dangers Pointed Out by the Ecology

The annual reports of the United Nations on the *State of the Environment* from 1974 to 1978 pointed to a number of major dangers with which the industrial civilisation is threatening Nature and, through Nature, mankind itself.

1. *The alteration in the oxygen layer.* Aerosols, chemical fertilisers, nuclear explosions and military and civil supersonic flights are possibly a serious threat to the atmospheric ozone layer (15-50 km above the earth's surface on average) which protects the life of man, of animals, of harvests, oceans and plankton from the ultraviolet rays. It is estimated that the ozone layer has already been reduced through the effect of dust clouds by at least 1% and will be by 10% in the year 2050 if the process is continued. A world nuclear war would have disastrous consequences in this respect: it could destroy by 20-70%

[1] Robert Allen, Towards an ecological strategy for Europe, in *The Promise of the Twentieth Century,* Round Table of the Council of Europe, 1974.

the vital screen formed by the ozone layer. The explosion (called 'excursion') of a fast-breeder reactor containing 4-5 tonnes of plutonium transformed into dust clouds dispersed throughout the planet by the atmospheric currents would be worse still, and would be *the last* explosion possible because there would be no survivors who would be ready to set off others. From various independent studies on the probable effects of a nuclear conflagration the conclusions can be drawn that:

(a) The damage would be so great—widespread, irreversible in most cases, unreal costs of restoring the radioactive cities and cultivated land, that *the whole of mankind could be mortally affected by it.* (The wheat from the United States which feeds 45% of the world would be contaminated; the cities of Western Europe swept by plutonium dust-clouds, tidal waves destroying millions of hectares of cultivated land, from which would come famine, epidemics, futile and murderous revolts, etc.)

(b) That consequently it is the immediate duty of the ecologists and all the scientists to recommend a policy calling for the destruction of nuclear armaments in all the countries which possess them, as well as the dismantling of the reactors ('conventional' or fast breeder) which would allow new countries to build them and to use them for terrorist activities. This would raise cries of 'Utopia' naturally, but is it 'realistic' to allow things to follow their present course towards final disaster?

It must also be added that the damage to the ozone layer will persist for 50 to 200 years after men have ceased from causing it.

2. *Cancer by the environment.* Cancer is recognised today as resulting from the fact that from 60% to 90% of our industrial environment is penetrated by 'half a million chemical substances', and this increases by 10,000 more every year. 'The majority are unquestionably cancer-inducing, above all in combinations, all of which cannot be tested.'[1]

3. *The loss of soil.* The surface of cultivated earth per inhabitant of our globe will have diminished by half by the end of the century. 600 million hectares of cultivable land will have deteriorated through

---

[1] *State of the Environment,* 1977, United Nations Organisation.

soil erosion, salinisation, urban expansion, while, at the same time, the world population will have doubled.

The revelation about this sterilisation of the soil, which is possibly the most sensational news item of the century, passed practically unnoticed. However, it is upon it that the policy of our generation should be based.

4. *The felling of trees* and the maintenance of fallow land opening the way to erosion (by wind and water) are the main causes of damage to the soil and later the famines from which whole populations will and already do suffer. This is the form which the energy crisis takes for all the world's poor. The total of felled trees is far higher than that of trees growing.[1] The world shrinkage of the forests is forcing millions of men and women to travel ever lengthening distances to warm themselves, while it enables the city-dwellers to glance at their newspapers, manufactured from the sacrificed trees.

The four phenomena described by the United Nations Report for 1977 appear to be linked together in so many ways that the Commission concluded that they were 'indissociables'. The only way to combat them is by close co-operation, interregional or intercontinental according to the case.

The first (reduced ozone-layer) affects all life on our planet. The second (cancer) affects primarily the industrialised world (the West and Japan). As for the third and fourth (loss of soil, forests destroyed) they mainly affect the Third World, but Europe will inevitably and rapidly suffer from their side-effects.

We must add the major dangers denounced by the UNO, those which concern more particularly Europe:

5. *The shortage of drinking water.* According to a study undertaken by the Economic Commission for Europe (the United Nations), the water in the rivers and the water-tables is already insufficient for the needs of several of our countries. Germany and Belgium are already importing water. While the reserves are diminishing, the demand is growing: we must fall back on salt water to cool our nuclear plants, which gives rise to new risks of ecological imbalance along a

---

The fossil combustibles (coal, oil, gas) represent 90% of the energy used in the whole world, wood only 6%. But in the Third World, as a whole, wood represents 28%, and in the African countries of the Southern Sahara, 75%.

coast line which is already fragile from this point of view. Lakes, rivers and streams are seriously threatened, on the other hand, by industrial pollution: the Rhine, 'the dustbin of Europe', discharges into the North Sea 60,000 tonnes of waste each day.

6. *Harmful agents in food* which denaturalise it under the pretext of 'conserving' it, that is to be able to sell it over a longer period. This in the first place concerns the subject of cancer, of rickets and of infant mortality.

7. *The extinction of animal and vegetable species.* In northern Europe: herrings, whales, the insects necessary to pollinisation, May-beetles, butterflies, etc. The Iberian peninsula and the Balkans still possess the richest flora in Europe, but in those two regions 200-300 species are threatened with extinction.

8. The uninhabitable conurbations of from 2 to 13 million inhabitants given over to the delinquency produced by polluted and polluting workers' blocks and devourers of energy (tower blocks, bottle-necks, neon advertising, etc.).

2. Nature of the Obstacles to the Necessary Measures

In most cases of pollution or of wastefulness, the cures or the preventive measures are known. But a succession of organic resistance, in our European-type societies, hampers their application or makes them inoperative.

Resistance from the industries. The reduction of pollution increases costs and delays in production. The policy of the large companies is therefore (a) to deny the damage (these are simply 'leftist nonsense'), (b) to minimise it, 'they are exaggerating', 'they are playing the Soviet game', 'our experts have shown'); (c) to get round governmental regulations; (d) to announce that 'from now on' precautions are being taken; (e) even to take some precautions; (f) but if the precautions prove to be too expensive, to export managers and machines, licences and pollution to countries where the regulations are less strict, or even non-existent—at the risk of creating unemployment in the country of origin and damage of the Seveso kind in the host country.

Resistance from the States. These play the same game except that instead of exporting pollution the State, which can no longer deny that it exists, assumes the costs of indemnification, then of the preventive measures, then the control of 'strict' rules drawn up by its own Minister for the Environment after ten or fifteen years during which the violations have become intolerable. This means that the costs of pollution are paid by the real or potential victims, that is the taxpayer, rather than by those who make it who must not be antagonised. As for the rest, the costs of recovering the lakes, rivers and coastlines, which have already been seriously affected, are so great that one can understand why the governments hesitate. To clean the Rhine basin, from Strasbourg to Rotterdam, for example, a milliard French francs per year would be needed. How could this sum be found in a budget which is already so heavily in debt to the firms which cause the pollution but who work on national defence?

Moreover, our governments, opposed to all kinds of ecological measures advocated by private or mixed, European or international organisations, anticipate a refusal from the very moment a communitarian solution (transfrontier, continental or worldwide) to the threats of the most common[1] or most dramatic[2] pollution threatens to infringe in any way the 'national sovereignty'. Our governments react like a patient who invokes *habeas corpus* to prevent a tooth from being pulled or when he is put in quarantine before he has carried the contagion to his neighbour.

The reasons for the *non-application* of the ecological measures taken by the governments, for the sabotage of the preventive measures against the effects of chronic pollution of every kind, or of the official *refusal* to co-operate on the international plane, all spring from the priority given to economic profits, on the one hand, and the 'needs of national defence', on the other.

This leads to the conclusion that the accumulated threats to Nature and the human environment from the industrial civilisation can only be overcome to the extent that the dogmas of private financial profit and the absolute sovereignty of the State can be overcome *in so much*

---

[1] Seas, rivers, subterranean water-tables; exported-imported feeding stuffs; and all the pollutions which cannot be stopped by political frontiers.

[2] 'Excursions' in the nuclear power plants situated near a frontier: sixteen power plants around the elbow of the Rhine at Basle, and the fast breeder reactor of Creys-Malville, 70 km from Geneva (to leeward) and 30 km from Lyons.

as they are deemed to be the ultimate criteria of all policy both social and military.

If Europeans do not very quickly succeed in understanding that realism lies in preventing the imminent eco-disasters, not in flattering the national vanity, then the present crisis is insoluble.

3. European Solutions

Links Between the Economy, Energy and the Ecology

These links are such that it would be imprudent to try to pursue simultaneously economic integration within the framework of the Nine or Twelve and the disintegration of the natural balances in the framework of national sovereignties.

Among the measures which are both ecological and economic which are unquestionably obligatory for our peoples we shall make a list— not exhaustive—of the ecological tasks which are most widely accepted as urgent and achievable.

1. The European Commission has asked its staff to draw up a *European water programme* which would allow it to intervene in some programme for the management of the waters which are of common interest to several different States. One of the first European tasks is in effect the salvaging of the polluted lakes, rivers and streams. (Example: Lake Geneva polluted by mercury and phosphorus and strongly eutrophised; the Rhine, polluted by five countries; estuaries transformed into airports and docks for oil tankers which lead to the destruction of the marine fauna, etc.

2. The fight against the growth of the *concentration of carbon dioxide* (CO_2) in the atmosphere, which could lead to the melting of the polar ice-caps and so to a rise in sea-level which could engulf all the harbour towns.

3. The protection of the *ozone layer* by the banning of aerosols, the restriction of supersonic flights and chemical fertilisers.

4. *Strict control of chemical products:* detergents, insecticides, colouring agents, preservatives in food products, etc.

5. *The renunciation of fast breeder reactors* in favour of sources of solar, wind, geothermal and biological energy. The option in favour of fast breeder reactors would in fact be irreversible: fast breeder

reactors would create tons of radioactive waste which would have to be treated and supervised until their activity became extinct, a process which nothing in the world can speed up by a single second. It is only too clear that no existing government could give an assurance that it would guarantee this stewardship for 240,000 years: no civilisation has ever lasted for more than 4000 years.

6. *The immediate halting of the production of new chemical substances* which it has not been shown through experiments that we can master the methods of eliminating them without damage to the environment or to people.

7. *The saving of animal species:* whales, seals, elephants, tigers, ocelots, etc., threatened by permanent extinction.

8. *A halt to the concretisation of the countryside.* Eighteen per cent of the soil in the Netherlands is already concreted and this will reach 25 % before the end of the century. What use will the motorways be when petrol costs twenty times more than it does today? An immediate start to research on a formula for a substitute for the car (and in consequence perhaps the motorways) should be one of the preemptive tasks of a federal European Authority.

9. *The adoption by all our countries of criteria of urbanism* designed to prevent the development of the cancerous atmosphere of the conurbations. (New cities of 50,000 inhabitants recommended by C. Doxiadis and by a number of modern urbanists; limitation of the number of storeys; streets and squares closed to traffic; free public transport.)

10. *The study of the climate, of the agents causing climatic modifications* and the conclusions to be drawn from it for our industries and our processes of energy production.

At the European level these measures imply *federal supranational* agreements which alone would be authorised to undertake the battle against pollution 'justified' by the calculations of local profit or 'authorised' by the absence of national laws regulating the production of the environment.

Once again, in this domain, it would seem from the evidence that the desirable solutions will only become possible through the continental union of our countries.

The first indispensable general measure being the normalisation of anti-pollution prescriptions in order to prevent the migration of the polluting industries to countries in which the regulations are less demanding in this respect (a process to which the multinationals habitually have recourse).

The second general measure being to entrust the continental Agencies with the distribution of ecological tasks according to their size, sometimes to the Federations, sometimes to the Regions.

From Energy to the Regions Through the Ecology
If these remedies are to work two basic conditions are called for:

(a) The formation of regional institutions, smaller than most of our national States and better adapted to local conditions, the diversity of which is one of the distinctive characteristics of Europe.

It is at the regional level, and there only, that this can be realised effectively: the ecological measures against the pollution of the waters (subterranean water-tables, lakes, rivers) for the production of solar, wind, geothermal or biological energy, for the protection of the soil and forests, for the defence of the landscape and monuments, etc.

(b) The formation of *federal Agencies* with continental powers alone authorised to plan very extensive measures: protection of the ozone layer, protection of the seas and international rivers; control of the food products which circulate through imports and exports in all our countries; banning of fast breeder reactors through international agreement; substitutes for the motor-car and the motorways; standardisation of the anti-pollution regulations.

These mixed institutions would be able to deal, for example, with problems of urbanisation, of the soil, of the seas or of the salvaging of the species.

These conditions for the realisation of measures which would preserve man, nature, towns and their balanced interrelations completely exclude the automatic recourse to 'absolute national sovereignty' and to the sacrosanct principle of 'non-interference', principles which, by the way, are ignored when pollution threatens a neighbouring country. Morality (and the usefulness for the greatest number) must take precedence over national selfishness and prestige which most of the time are misunderstood.

Mankind of today and tomorrow cannot accept that the States should invoke their 'sovereignty' in order to evade their vital ecological obligations under the pretext that these are most often according to their nature and dimensions continental, across frontiers, or regional.

Change of Course

To be sure, this does not mean that all the people in our countries should become learned ecologists. What the present crisis urgently needs is that the most civically aware men and women in Europe should get used to *subordinating* material 'progress' to moral well-being, the immediate profit of some to the opportunities for happiness of every-one, the 'national defence' to peace, energy to the aims of the work which it is supposed to serve; and the nationalistic myths to everyday realities.

It is very unlikely that the measures recommended in this Report will be applied by the governments if they are not forced to do so by serious accidents, which are already inevitable, and by the will of the citizens, as far as they can give expression to it, notably in the elections to the European Parliament.

In assuming their rights as well as their duties on the local scale, and by voting for the candidates who are most aware of the ecological and regional situation, our peoples still possess effective means to shape the only possible future for Europe.

4

The Regions

1. Emergence of the Problem

Simultaneous Birth of the Regions and of the European
Federation

The Region is probably the most important political novelty of the century since the appearance at the end of the First World War of the totalitarian States of Stalin, Mussolini and Hitler, which were imitated after the Second World War by nearly fifty one-party dictatorships in Europe first and then, after decolonisation, in Africa, Latin America and Asia.

The Region can be explained as a reaction against the centralising frenzy which is characteristic of the totalitarian States and represents the final stage in the evolution of the Nation-State which was born of the French Revolution and the Napoleonic Empire.

From 1792 to the 1960s we saw a gradual reduction, which was generally considered progressive, of linguistic minorities, of the systematic dissolution of ethnic communities, of the suppression of local and regional liberties, of the growing subordination of man, of his values and his desires to the ambitions, called necessities or 'raisons d'Etat' by the political, administrative or military apparatuses which had succeeded in taking over a nation. The totalitarian dictatorships put the finishing touch to this process. They killed, perhaps for a long time, every kind of vitality, of civic spontaneity.

It was then in the least 'advanced' in this respect and the most liberal (that is the least brutally oppressive) Nation-States that the first reactions could be seen of the ethnic communities and 'minorities' of every kind who felt that they ought to protest and make their voices heard wherever it was still possible and wherever it was not already too late.

It must be emphasised that the first regionalist claims followed closely upon the setting up of the first organisations for European union: notably the creation of the Common Market, then the unification of the three economic Communities (ECSC, Euratom and the Common Market) under the initials of the EEC, established in Brussels (from 1958 to 1967). The link between the two phenomena is obvious: it was only necessary for there to appear on the horizon the possibility of an Authority superior to those of the States and capping their 'indivisible sovereignties' for the hope to be reborn that local and regional facts should be taken seriously. Neither of these two movements could prosper without the other; in reality they are the two apparently contradictory but in practice inseparable aspects of the overtaking of the Nation-State structure from below and above at the same time, that is to say by the Regions as basic elements of the continental Federation.

At the same time as a 'general Directorate for Regional Policy' was created in Brussels the first regionalist claims were heard in many Western European countries. (Nothing, or practically nothing, is known about the clandestine activities of the regionalists in eastern Europe.) In France, plastic bombs in Brittany and Corsica; in Great Britain a Scottish and Welsh movement demanding the 'devolution' of the central power to the regional authorities; in Italy, agitation for the enforcement of the Constitution voted after the fall of fascism which made provision in the Peninsula for the creation of twenty regions with real powers. In Spain, a dark series of assassinations in the Basque country, growing pressure of the Catalan movement, demanding the return to the status of autonomy before Franco; in Switzerland agitation and plastic bombs in the French-speaking and Catholic Jura 'attributed' since 1814 to the German and Protestant canton of Berne.

In all these countries everyone was in agreement in condemning the plastic bombers and violence in general. But one very important distinction must be made between the acts of violence against the TV networks, the police cars (empty), even a room in a history museum lauding the victories of a tyrant, on the one hand, and the murder of people like those committed by the increasing number of some 'nationalist' movement in Northern Ireland or in the Basque country.

The first were *symbolic* gestures committed by the autonomists who complained that they had not the means to make themselves heard by the public and to compel the governments to pay heed to them. The second were *crimes* not only against the established order, often held to be oppressive, but against the order *to be established,* against the cause itself in the name of what they were claiming to fight. It has rightly been said that the terrorist crimes committed by ETA pose the worst threat at present, not only against Spanish democracy but against regionalism in itself, against the federalist spirit, against Europe, against liberty in the world of tomorrow.

Claims and Motivations

It remains to be seen what their *claims* are (those which they declare) and what are the profound motivations (not always completely conscious) which inspire their struggle. Three kinds of claims correspond to three types of regions.

(a) The awakening of ethnic peoples, historical groups and linguistic minorities engulfed against their will more often than not by a national State which tended to suppress their identity and to eliminate so far as possible their cultural, legal, economic and social characteristics in proportion as centralisation became more demanding in all spheres. Examples: Scotland, Wales, Brittany, the Basque country, Catalonia, Languedoc, Corsica, South Tyrol, Val d'Aosta, Alsace, Flanders, the Jura, etc. Their grievances and claims are always the same: the right to their own historic language in all sectors of public life (schools, councils, courts, media, publications), suppression of all kinds of discrimination (economic as well as cultural and social) of which they say they are the victims and which the dominant ethnic group uses for its own benefit in the national State (Castilian, French, English, Walloon, Piedmontese, Lombard, etc.); this dominant ethnic group imposes not only its language, called 'literary', on the 'dialects' of the conquered people, but also its own system of values.[1]

---

[1] The French imposed on the "Occitanie" of the Troubadours was still only a military, not a literary language. Later the conquering ethnic group described as 'dialects' the older and richer languages of the 'conquered nations'. *'What is a language? It is a dialect plus an army'*, said W. Sombart.

(b) Other regions, like the Mezzogiorno, Sardinia, the south-west of France or the Polar Circle, are described as essentially economic problems—those in the charge of the General Directorate of the regional policy of the Community. Ethnic claims play hardly any part at all in it.

(c) Many cross-frontier groupings represent a third category: sometimes deprived of historical unity but speaking the same language or similar dialects across the frontiers which actually separate our Nation-States. These regions are defined by common reactions to certain socio-economic challenges or to some threats to their environment which help to form a regional consciousness and the sense of a common destiny among their people.

This is how the *Regio basiliensis* aimed at grouping the Alsacians (French) and the Badois (German) and the Bâlois (Swiss) who live on the banks of the Rhine and speak very similar German dialects was formed with the immediate aims of reducing the pollution of the atmosphere and of the river, of improving public transport and the conditions of the workers on the frontiers, of creating a common international airport and of resisting the building around the elbow of the Rhine of sixteen nuclear power plants (six parts French, five parts Swiss, and five parts German) which to say the least are superfluous to the real needs of the region.

About fifteen other regions provoked by similar problems and the possibilities of the same kind of solution are being formed from the Northern Cape (Norway, Sweden, Finland) to Friesland and as far as Basle. About ten of them cross over the common frontiers with Germany, Denmark, Holland, Belgium, Luxembourg, France and Switzerland. Some contain districts from three different countries, as, for example, the regions of Aix-la-Chapelle-Liège-Maastricht and Saar-Lorraine-Luxembourg; the region called Lémano-Alpine which is formed astride the French-Swiss frontier around Geneva; lastly the region which can be called Triestine: Frioul-Carinthia-Slovenia, at the extreme east of the Alpine arc.

Some of these claims (especially those of the ethnic groups) were made by reactionary elements at the beginning of the century, and the governments of the Nation-States all tended to direct them towards folklore, historic commemorations and local erudition. This was how in France the Félibrige, an essentially cultural movement created in Provence by Frederic Mistral (who received one of the first Nobel prizes for literature), was encouraged by Paris. But after the Second World War, when the European, that is supra-national, horizon appeared, the regional claims throughout the whole of Europe rapidly took a new turn. It was no longer so much the past and the collective symbols that were to be preserved, but the future, civil liberties and concrete responsibilities which were to be restored or established. The regionalist cause, without loss of its traditional tenets, became an *avant-garde* cause, mobilising the Left and Leftist youth as much as the Right.

(d) Behind all the claims which have been mentioned, the *need for civil participation* is unquestionably the most fundamental motivation common to all the types of regions.

This need can of itself be enough, in the absence of ethnic 'problems' and economic challenges, to give rise to regional problems without historical precedents (at least conscious), aimed at a future in which a man can once again make his voice heard, and act as a citizen who is both free and responsible in a community of human size.

For it is here only that the citizen can see and judge the effective import of the decisions to which he has contributed:

— about the creation or the maintenance of paid employment or craft activities;
— about the local production and the distribution of solar, hydraulic, wind, geothermal, biological energy;
— about the protection of the soil, of the humus, of forests, waters, the air;
— about public transport;
— about the holding in common of agricultural implements, of bodies and of minds when they overstep the possibilities of the individual, of the family or of the commune.

Such regions, described as *spaces of civil participation,* are being created even where there is no ethnic or linguistic problem and no economic challenge to characterise them.

We have seen the case of the *Regio basiliensis*; everyone there speaks the same real although not official language in the Alsace part. But in the Lémano-Alpine region this is not so, and there in reality remain only motivations of common action on the civic plane within a given territory. The same is true for the majority of the regions of the *Communidades autónomas* drawn up in the Spanish Constitution: with the exception of Catalonia and the Basque country they do not correspond to linguistic or ethnic particularities but only to the needs, indicated by their name, of the community and of autonomy. They spring, then, from the most generalised definition of the Region as a space of civil participation.

Other regions, all English, are appearing in the Midlands, all Italians in the Boot of Italy; it is possible that other all French will appear in the Centre, the Southwest, the Franche Comté.

It appears thus that the regional phenomenon in its totality draws its essential motivations from a reaction against the advance of stato-national centralisation, a more profound reaction than all the isolated or combined ethnic or economic claims.

The proof of this can be seen in the fact that many Swiss cantons are bilingual, and one is even quadrilingual, without any grave political or economic problems having resulted from this plurality: this is because the German, French, Italian, Ladines or Romanches linguistic communities who live together in the cantons of Friburg, of the Valais and of the Grisons on an unquestionably equal footing have always been able to *participate genuinely* in the public decisions of their State. And it is true that their reunion with other ethnic groups to form a canton ('a sovereign State', according to the Swiss Constitution) was the outcome of a free common decision. The reverse happened in the case of the Jura: in 1814 this country found itself 'attributed' by the Great Powers to the State of Berne, a country with a different language and religious faith. Hence the *separatist* movement (and not merely autonomist) which arose in the 1950s and which has just reached its goal in the creation of a new Cantonal State: if the ethnic and economic claims were decisive on this occasion, it was precisely because, unlike what took place in the other bilingual cantons, the people of the Jura 'attributed' to Berne did not feel that they were masters of their own destiny.

What Has Been Done Up to Now

In Europe everything begins with congresses, including revolutions. And the 'regionalist revolution', as it has already been called, is no exception.

In Brussels, in 1961, the *Conference on the Regional Economies* appeared to be the first official recognition of the regional theme on the European plane. Spontaneous initiatives, grouping together economists, industrialists, sociologists, members of parliament, and local deputies, answered in several countries this sign that the debate was about to begin, while the 'General Directorate of Regional Policy' created by the Brussels Community was paralleled since 1970 by the European Conference of the Local and Regional Authorities of the Council of Europe. The latter called in Strasbourg in 1972 a first European Confrontation of the Frontier Regions.[1]

During these meetings, which now take place regularly, the delegates from the Regions which are being formed can compare their problems, their methods, their solutions. They discover that while each Region presents unique traits, it is in this that they most resemble each other. They are emerging from their long, sometimes despairing struggle in retreat to enter a great continental movement of renewal.

To these congresses sponsored by the intergovernmental organisations were added the very numerous colloquia organised by the European federalists, by the University Institutes for European Studies (there are forty of them) and recently by the ecological movements concerned to mark their decisive convergence with the federalist and regionalist movements.

Around these colloquia, each of which marked an advance towards the synthesis of the forces emerging 'for Europe', proliferate thousands of works of research, volumes, special numbers of periodicals which in turn feed the regional weeklies and newspapers, manifestoes, tracts and bulletins, all this translating the growing reality of a pheno-

---

[1] Behind the moderation of European diplomatic language, always obsessed by a religious respect for absolute national sovereignty and which considers that any federalist trend is indecent, *confrontation* must be taken to mean *co-operation* and *frontier regions* to mean *transfrontier regions*. This is what has been understood up to now by the participants in the meetings which have followed that of 1972—Innsbruck 1974, Galway 1976, Bordeaux 1978.

menon which only the apparatus of the political parties still pretend to cast doubt on and which is none other than the urgent need to decentralise to the maximum, to regionalise and to localise the political and economic powers if we want to save Europe from the disaster of industrial societies, from their gigantism, from the basic lack of appreciation of the true needs of mankind, as well as of the natural rhythms and equilibria.

2. Crisis of the Centralist State

But at the level of the Nation-State and of their governments, it must be recognised that the resistance of the national administrations and of the politicians to any redistribution of the powers of the central State still dominates the situation.

The vastness of the regionalist movement is still not perceived by the public of our countries, which only wakes up when it hears the noise of plastic bombs exploding periodically, destroying the symbols of the centralised State: police cars or transmitters of the speeches of the capital.

The apparatus of the big parties, with two or three exceptions, appears reticent or frankly hostile.

Some fear the Regions because of a Jacobin egalitarianism which sees in every 'difference' a threat of dissidence and in every recognised particularism a potential 'privilege'. Others comdemn all *real* decentralisation in the name of a system of capitalist 'efficiency' which has been tested they tell us. (Is this by inflation and unemployment?)

All see in a Europe of the Regions a return to chaos or, what seems worse to them, to feudalism (although they know nothing of its structures and functions in the Middle Ages).

Whereas it is the present centralisation which creates crises of every kind—economic, social, educational, political, and the violence which result from them.

The most serious chaos is that which war brings about. Now it cannot be denied that the wars in Europe for a century have all been sparked off by problems which were either unresolved or brutally denied to the Regions. From Schleswig-Holstein in 1864, to the Sudeten Germans in 1939, including Alsace-Lorraine in 1870 and Bosnia in

1914. This is to say that they were all caused by the obdurate rejection of any kind of federalist solution, of any real recognition of the right of the people to free self-determination within a freely consented union.

Today, the dominant trend in Europe can be seen by the opposition to the totalitarian regimes (successively Greece, Portugal, Spain, have liquidated their dictatorships without bloodshed) by the affirmation everywhere reiterated of the advantages of decentralisation. We have also seen our leading States reaffirming at every turn their determination to sacrifice none of their 'absolute and indivisible national sovereignty', while repeating their determination 'to increase the unity between the European nations'. But *these two determinations are contradictory in theory and in practice.*

Scientific objectivity forces us to say that:

(1) The governments of the States which are most sensitive about safeguarding their national independence are also those which for several centuries have constantly refused to give any rights of 'independence', even of simple autonomy, to the peoples conquered and annexed by their ancestors, for example:

— in France: Brittany, the Basque country, Occitanie, Catalan
   Roussillon, Provence, Corsica, Alsace;
— in Great Britain: Scotland, Wales, Cornwall, Northern Ireland.

(2) It is perverse to claim to found the union of Europe on States which are so jealous of the smallest particle of their independence and which nevertheless internally only think of union in the form of a forcible assimilation of the weakest by the strongest.

Hence, unquestionably, the perpetual fear of these same States of the 'risks of hegemony' within a European union of any Nation-State other than their own. They cannot imagine that a united Europe will not treat them as they themselves have treated their 'nations' (in the old meaning of the word: ethnic groups, languages). They are the most eloquent in claiming at the European level respect for independence and identity—even those which they have degraded internally at the national level.

This situation can only portend an escalation of violence unless new solutions are found quickly. But here again they can only be European ones.

For as an already classic analysis has shown us, the Nation-States of Europe are in crisis for two reasons:

— they are too small to play an effective part on the world scale or to guarantee their own defence;
— they are too large (with two or three exceptions) to give real life to their Regions and to solve their problems of unemployment and ecology education.

Why is this? Because our Nation-States, being born of war, continue to find in preparation for war, called 'national defence', the justification in the last resort, the *ultima ratio* of their least defensible decisions from every other point of view—whether they be economic, ecological, cultural or simple justice: nuclear power plants (ruinously expensive), sales of armaments and research on bacteriological warfare (criminal), priority given to the industries which are most closely linked to armaments (and so much the worse for the activities which nourish mankind), etc.

The Nation-State being the main obstacle not only to its own regionalisation (internal federalism) but also to any integration in the European continental ensemble (external federation), it is clear that the Region and European Federation cannot come into being without each other: no European Federation without the Region as basic units, no viable Regions without an opening on the European Federation, and through this on the united world—the ultimate objective.

3. European Solutions

To Start Again from Below

'There will never be real liberty for the citizen so long as the collectivities of which they are part have not themselves become fully responsible.'[1]

---

[1] Guy Héraud, *L'Europe en formation,* October-November 1975.

'We are going to try to humanise professional life and strengthen the individual's participation in the local and provincial communities. Our programme is to be found in one word: decentralisation.'[1]

'The Nation-State is no longer the ultimate criterion of policy in our country.'[2]

These three declarations describe very clearly the conditions for any restoration or creation of efficient and peaceful communities wherever Napoleonic centralism has obviously failed.

The trend must be reversed: instead of deciding everything from an administrative centre deaf to political directives, whatever they may be and no matter from how high they come,[3] we must start from the bottom, from local groups and communities—with their immense force of germination.

To start from the bottom, that is to say from the smallest units, means exactly what it says, what the American diplomat D. Moynihan said recently about the United States, but which it is easy to translate into European terms: *'Never entrust to a large unit what can be done by a smaller one. The municipality must not do what the family can do. Governments must not do what the municipality can do. And the federal government must not do what the States can do.'*

Most European sociologists and political scientists and many responsible politicians in the United States agree: the decentralisation of the government, of the economy and of cultural activities seems to them the very condition of a civic, economic cultural renaissance in their countries.

Spectacular Progress, Sometimes

Apart from wars of aggression and nuclear power plants, which both demand a jealous centralisation, *everything* works better on a small scale within local autonomies. 'Housing co-operatives, solar energy, small businesses, compost, the food industry, local banks: neighbourhoods begin to find again the sense of their autonomy, to

---

[1] Th. Fälldin, Swedish Prime Minister, *Le Monde,* 7 December 1976.
[2] Helmut Schmidt, Speech to the Assembly of the Council of Europe, April 1978.
[3] Cf. *Le mal francais,* by Alain Peyrefitte, Paris, 1977.

take their fate back into their own hands.'[1] It is not true that the biggest is the most efficient. E. M. Schumacher has shown decisively that the contrary is true in his book *Small is Beautiful.* Here, again, our best European sociologists and political scientists endorse this point of view enthusiastically, but it is seldom they are followed other than by words by influential politicians such as State governors and mayors of the great conurbations who in America fight for local autonomy and trans-State regions.

However, the progress is noticeable, sometimes spectacular, not only in the awareness of the regional phenomenon but already in the drawing up of measures to restore the autonomy of the Regions, especially in Italy, Spain, Great Britain and Belgium (see Appendix III).

This evolution seems to be the preliminary to any continental formation of a genuine *Europe of the Regions.* Because it is almost impossible to federate entities anything but federative given the fact that the centralists oppose it by virtue of their very principle.

The main actors in the federation of the Regions can be divided into four classes: States on the way to federalist decentralisation (see Appendix I); the European intergovernmental organisations (Council of Europe, Economic Community); the trans-frontier Regions already operational or about to become so; the federalist movements and the ecological movements.

The States on the way to internal federalisation are preparing to go beyond the national sovereignties in favour of the regional communities—basic units of any federation.

The economic communities make it conceivable that the notions of mutual aid could replace competition and that of equalisation replace the exploitation of the poorest by the richest.

The Council of Europe, through its Conference of Local and Regional Authorities, launched the idea of a European Senate of the Regions: this is until now the most daring and innovating initiative ever shown at the level of intergovernmental organisations.

Lastly, the trans-frontier Regions are the forefront of the struggle for Europe, the place of the decisive battle between federalism and stato-nationalism. A silent breakthrough has taken place, still unper-

[1] The *Ecologist,* special issue on the *Future of America,* September 1977.

ceived perhaps happily by the mass media and the politicians: this is the *Franco-Swiss Consultative Commission,* appointed in 1975 by the governments in Berne and Paris to deal with a growing number of problems each year affecting the population of the canton of Geneva, Haute Savoie and the Pays de Gex. This innovation, which will be seen as a precedent, heralds a coming development of trans-frontier administrative entities: it thus has historical value. Already the *Regio basiliensis* is a similar case, with this time a tripartite commission. The way is open to the superseding of the absolute and indivisible national sovereignties as the way to federation, one might say the only formula for union which can be accepted without the reaction of rejection by our thirty European countries, and even more by the immense diversity of their Regions.

4. Requisite Conditions

If this way is to lead to practical results in good time, some conditions are required:

(1) That the inhabitants of the Regions should understand that they are not to be granted powers by the central State nor to 'take power' in the capital, but to form themselves into regional powers on the spot with direct means through the initiatives of deprived groups from the start. When these means of action have been tested it will be time enough to have them recognised by agreements with other neighbouring Regions, national States, European Authorities.

(2) That those who are responsible for the government of the regional policy should have a world vision and not a sectorial (self-interested) or national one of the problems of the modern world; that they should be bold enough to announce clearly and simply in the official declarations the necessity—recognised, although not always publicly, by everyone—to go beyond the dogma of absolute national sovereignty: all the technological, ecological, socio-economic and monetary realities have already done so in fact, as for hundreds of years in Europe have the spiritual, cultural and scientific realities.

(3) That a system of taxation transformed in function and for the benefit of local needs should at last provide the indispensable financial means to the regional autonomy.

(4) That the Press, radio, TV and schools should take every opportunity of emphasising daily everything which illustrates not the superiority of 'our country' but our now obvious evident interdependence and our felicitous complementaries.

In this way will be linked the chain of realities which call for the union of the peoples of Europe: Ecology—Regions—Federation: One Future.

5

European Defence

1. State of the Question

European defence is a subject which has been avoided in the public debate of recent years and one on which no one seems to be prepared to give a frank opinion. This is either out of humanitarian scruples or through nationalistic pride, partisan calculation,[1] or simply through reluctance to face up to the 'unthinkable', a third world war which this time would really be the last because of the power of the armaments which today mankind can use against itself.

Yet it is this aspect of the European problem which today most concerns the people if the public opinion polls are to be believed.

This is the source of the contradiction between the real anxiety of the peoples and the speeches of the politicians which are, to say the least, ambiguous.

2. The failure of the proposal for a *European Defence Community* caused incalculable damage to the cause of European union. The EDC was proposed by French statesmen and accepted by all the other countries of the Common Market. It was finally rejected by the French Parliament alone, as a result of a coalition between the Gaullists and the communists, in the name of the alleged fear that a German contingent would be integrated into the European forces and of the necessity to safeguard 'sovereignty', and 'national independence' in face of the 'self-interested aid of the Americans'.

---

[1] The nationalist Right did not agree to 'be dependent on the Americans' while counting on their help; the Left feared to irritate the masters of the USSR while knowing that the only danger might come from them.

The consequences of the rejection of the EDC were twofold:

(1) the immediate rebirth of an independent (i.e. not integrated) German army;
(2) increased dependence on the United States for nuclear defence.

That was exactly what the federalists had wanted to avoid when they proposed the EDC and the nationalists when they rejected it.

Ever since, the *European plans* proposed by the politicians (Fouchet, Harmel, Davignon, Tindemans) as well as by NATO and by the Euro-group have all been rejected by the European Council of Ministers in the name of the Nation-States, members of the European Community.

This would not have been possible without the indestructible confidence of the immense majority of the Europeans (including the Gaullists and Eurocommunists) in the automatic opening of the 'American umbrella', no matter what might happen, however impertinent some political leaders would like to show themselves to Jimmy Carter, persuaded as they are that the President will pay no attention to their swashbuckling speeches or that he will understand that they are only trying to win applause at party congresses.

If these leaders, and above all their troops, realised the precarious state of our national non-integrated forces, the rapidly increasing superiority of the Russian forces and uncertainty of an American nuclear intervention, they would no longer be contented with the alibi of the 'umbrella'; they would see clearly the need to unite at least enough to set up a common defence of the whole continent—and the rest would follow as a natural consequence, providing that it was done in such a way that there was an army following.

There remain the reasons for the dependence on the Americans of a Europe of States clearly unable to plan its own defence by its own means. These reasons are roughly as follows:

(a) The crushing superiority of the USSR over all our non-integrated countries as the sole nuclear force engaged in the European region: the potentiality is 1 (France and Great Britain) to 15 (USSR).
(b) The crushing superiority of the Warsaw Pact (imposed by Moscow on its satellites) over the Europe of the Nine and even

over NATO (France left of its own accord) in conventional forces:

	NATO	Warsaw Pact
Forces	626,000 (285,000 of whom are American)	943,000
Tanks	7,000	21,000
Artillery	2,700	10,000
Planes	2,375	4,055

And this in spite of the fact that the populations are practically equal on either side of the Iron Curtain.[1]

(c) The flagrant lack of unity of the Europeans when faced not only with their defence problems but with the question of what they should defend as a priority: national sovereignty, the capitalist system, or civil liberties, such as the right to oppose, to strike, professional mobility, free international travel, private property, etc.?

The question of *the defence of Europe should no longer be a question of figures*: number of ground-to-ground or ground-to-air weapons of different types of bombs. The people cannot understand this and are rightly losing interest in it: what use are armaments if the will to use them is lacking?

Why (they ask vaguely) is 373 milliard dollars per year spent on armaments in the world? One lot has the means to kill the other 33,000 times; the other only 30,000 times. What sense is there in this rivalry?

This is at the root of the striking weakness of the motivations which can be seen among our people when it comes to a common defence of some vague kind of Europe, although the isolated defence of one of our countries alone would seem to be a laughable claim, whether it is a question of the GFR, of Luxembourg, even of France or Great Britain.

---

[1] Western Europe: *395 millions.* USSR: 260 millions plus Eastern Europe: 12ö millions, total *388 millions.*

2. The Crisis

Competent and independent-minded military authors who have dealt with the problem of the global defence of Europe against a massive attack from the East (the only eventuality imaginable today)— any aggression by one of our countries on the USSR being excluded for reasons of size just as for political reasons any aggression by a federated Europe is also excluded—have come up with radically pessimistic conclusions if Europe persists in remaining disunited.

Among the numerous scenarios let us quote first the case of two generals who have both held important positions in NATO. That of General Robert Close, commander of a Belgian tank division, who was director of studies at the NATO Defence College. And that of the German General Johannes Steinhoff, who was president of the military committee of the Atlantic Alliance in Brussels.

(a) The first, in *L'Europe sans défense?*,[1] described a surprise attack by the Russians who succeeded in a few hours in joining up their airborne troops and their armoured divisions in the GFR. After this, messages and threats were exchanged between the Pentagon and the Kremlin, the latter being ready to stop the operation if the other yielded. Threats, confusion, consultations, thanks to which the Russians were on the Rhine in 48 hours: this was the time needed for the American President to decide whether or not to use nuclear weapons. The Russians possess the bulk of the forces of production in Europe: is the victory not already won?

What is certain is that at present 'the destruction or the salvation of Europe rests entirely in the hands of a Head of State who, no matter how favourable he may be to Western views, is not a European and represents world interests, some of which may be appreciably different from ours' (R. Close, op. cit., p. 283).

(b) General Steinhoff, unlike the French General P. Gallois, does not believe that 'each nation, in imitation of France, can guarantee its own defence'. (What would Luxembourg do?, he asks.) Above all, he does not believe that 'the Americans would fly to the help of the Europeans' unable to unite: 'Why should we go and die for Frankfurt

---

[1] General Robert R. Close, *L'Europe sans défense?*, Editions Arts et Voyages, Brussels, 1977.

or Düsseldorf, when the Europeans do so little for their own security?'[1] The Americans will only protect the Europeans if the latter show their common will to defend themselves. 'Demography, common shared cultural heritage, industrial, and technological power', all urge this. But if they do not want to unite, 'This time I agree with Close.' (The Russians on the Rhine in 48 hours.)

(c) The British and French 'atomic weapons of dissuasion' have been put forward as a counter-argument. The reply of most of the military writers and critics: the atomic weapon of any European nation would be unusable:

— against another European country or against foreign troops invading Europe; anyone dropping it on his neighbour would be at the mercy of a change of wind;
— against a surprise attack from the East, for 'the speed of the action, the penetration in depths of the enemy forces—closely mingled with the civilian population—makes it inconceivable to use nuclear weapons which would cause more losses among the civilian populations than among the aggressors (General Close);
— lastly, to 'dissuade' the USSR, whose total nuclear arsenal is one hundred times greater than our own.

But this is the most important point: even with nuclear parity, Europe would be the loser because the extreme density of its population, of its cities, of its factories, its art treasures and monuments, of its communications network, etc., makes it infinitely more vulnerable than the USSR with its vast empty plains.[2] A few Russian bombs on the capital and on the power centres would be enough to paralyse any of our European countries, whereas all the bombs produced by that country or given to it by the USA would do no more than inconvenience the USSR, even supposing that they had not been neutralised in the first few minutes of the conflict or immediately after.

By slightly exaggerating the situation, one could say that it is not even certain that if a united Europe had at its disposal the huge Russian

---

[1] Interview by General Steinhoff, *Construire*, 29 June 1977, Lausanne.
[2] Density of population to the square kilometre: in the USSR 11, in Western Europe 127.

nuclear force, it could do as much damage to the USSR as the latter could inflict on her with the small French and British nuclear force.

It seems that a national striking force can only lead to the useless and definitive crushing of a densely populated industrial country after having been used as a poor excuse by the nationalists of that country to reject a European Defence Council alone able to cope with the danger.

If therefore we are unwilling to allow 'the destruction or salvation of Europe to rest in the hands of an American Head of State' we are condemned to *invent* a different future, above all in the realm of defence.

And here again we can only find the solution in union provided that this union is federal.

3. The Defence of Europe Will Be the Work of the Europeans Themselves

Whatever the imagined or imaginable scenarios may be, with or without 'the Americans', with or without nuclear weapons, nothing can withstand the following evidence:

— Nuclear weapons are offensive in their nature and can only be used to make war on the other—even although the attack is described as preventative. Nuclear weapons are of their nature unsuited to the defence of our countryside, our cities, our populations, our soldiers at grips with the invaders and, in general, of the civilisation of the European continent which their use would destroy.[1]

— 'The Americans' will not risk a nuclear war if the Europeans do not show their will to defend themselves by their will to unite.

— A genuine defence of Europe would consist in safeguarding our cities, our countryside, our customs, our cultures. We must first love them. There is no effective and sound defence without an awareness of what Europe means for our daily lives.

But to defend a country without destroying the reasons one has for loving it is to defend first of all one's birthplace—not the invisible

---

[1] With the exception of the tactical neutron bomb used against tanks.

frontiers, nor a government which one only knows through its con-
straints. It is a question of Regions, not of States.

Now the tactics which correspond to the defence of human realities, not the national-State-controlled myths, are called in military
terms hedgehog tactics—local defence, village by village. Local fight-
ing, which is the truly motivated form. Each man defends his own
land, his own family, his material and affective riches. Each man
defends his liberties and with much greater conviction than the man
who attacks him because he has been forced to do so.

It is this form of defence which General Close has rightly called
'popular dissuasion', which we have seen in other parts of the world
defeating the most powerful army in the world. It faces the enemy
with the choice between a 'costly conquest or futile destruction'.
(Raymond Aron.)

To conquer a country village by village, house by house is very
costly and of little value. But to defend a country in the same way is
not only the most profitable, which would be of little avail, but is
above all the most uplifting for the morale of the population.

This tactic, the only one suitable to the topography, demography,
sociology and the diversity of our continent, presupposes and favours
an authentic and spontaneous will to defend which nothing in the
world can replace.

The defence capacity of Europe depends, above all, on the will of
the Europeans to defend their liberties, their civil rights and duties. It
depends thus on the opportunities which the institutions will bring
to the rebirth of the Regions, that is to say, the territorial units whose
dimensions will permit the real exercise of its liberties, of its rights
and of its duties.

The vitality of the Regions, in turn, depends upon the jealous
upholding of its respect for its diversities. Respect which can only
lead—logically and practically—to neutrality as the refusal to have
recourse to violence to resolve a difference.

The European Federation would be neutral because of the impos-
sibility—due to its too great diversities—of deciding upon a policy of
aggression against any neighbour whatsoever—Russian or from the
Maghreb, Arab or African.

The vital interest of a federated Europe in and for its regional diversities, a neutral Europe, would be to recommend and to initiate *world disarmament*.[1]

The problem of defence is inseparable from that of disarmament just as that of energy is inseparable from that of the reduction of wastefulness.

Today there is a wastefulness of armaments (what use is it to be able to kill 3,000 or 33,000 times over all human beings?) and energetic over-armament in Europe.

Just as the reduction in the wasteful use of energy would soon become the main source of available energy (according to the Director of the International Energy Agency, UNO, in Vienna), so disarmament would be the main reinforcement for our defence.

But Europe can only contribute towards general disarmament if it shows that it is united and that its union shows that it is capable of giving the world something other than selfish advice, i.e. a living example of atomic disarmament (towards which every known reason urges it).

United Europe can alone begin the de-escalation of armaments without which there is no future for our history.

---

[1]In a preliminary phase in which the States would still continue to exist alone and absolute (or at least would claim to be so), the simplest formula would be to make armaments inversely proportionate to the population—surface quotient of a State. Thus the USSR would be, because of its surface and its population density, less armed than Holland. But this is only a possibly illuminating fancy.

6

Europe and the Third World

1. The Problems

The civilisation which has been developed and which the Europeans—explorers, missionaries and traders, then colonisers—exported to the Americas, to Asia and to Africa, produced in those continents in the twentieth century some phenomena, signs of a far too rapid evolution not to cause disquiet, in spite of all the 'progress' in Western terms that they represent:

— *a population explosion* the main known features of which are at present the decline in infant mortality, the elimination of widespread epidemics and the reduction of infectious diseases, thanks to Western medicine and pharmacology;

— owing to contact with European culture through the schools and colonial administrations, the discovery of machines and techniques, travel and television, a *widespread desire to imitate Western ways of life* without distinguishing any better than we have between their advantages and their harmful effects;

— at the same time a *desire to copy the political models and the economic aims of the colonising States,* believing that by so doing they can liberate themselves and affirm their independence.

In this way some eighty Nation-States of all sizes have been created since the end of the Second World War, successors to the former European colonies in South-East Asia, the Middle East, and Africa. Among them one-party régimes and military dictatorships are the rule, the democracies the exception.

'The ideal' of industrial development has been adopted by these new States even more rashly and uncritically than by the Western Europeans.

This is the reason for the remarkable convergence between the desire for industrial development affirmed as a fundamental and overriding right of their people by the leaders of the new States; and the desire which the West proclaims to aid this development by all the means at the disposal of well-ordered charity: the charity which begins at home. For the Third World the West represents mastery of the scientific-technological methods thanks to which oil, for example, which was nothing under the desert sands, has become the fabulous wealth of the Arabs and the vital fluid of Western industry. Similar transformations have produced gold from copper or from uranium, from wood, from the pelts of seals or even from cheap labour which enables the European multinationals, which export technology, to make profits which are far higher than the costs to the European taxpayers of the unemployment they cause at home.

If these are the basic facts of the problem of the relations between Europe and the Third World, what can be the future of the development in which both are equally in every sense of the word *interested*?

2. The Worldwide Crisis

After the 'oil crisis' which followed soon after the Yom Kippur war in the autumn of 1973, some of the conflicts latent in the above situation emerged dramatically.

First, it was revealed that the accelerated exploitation of the non-renewable resources of the Third World (hydrocarbons and minerals) were already showing signs of exhaustion in the relatively near future, depriving future generations in not only the West but the whole of the Third World. Professors from the Massachusetts Institute of Technology explained to the Third World that it must abandon any hope of ever reaching the present standard of living in the Western countries: there was simply not enough oil, steel, aluminium and copper in the whole world to manufacture the quantities of motor-cars, planes, telephones and plastic objects needed for such a 'development'.

Then it was revealed that the 'victories' won by the pesticides manufactured in Europe had unlocked the floodgates in the Third World, letting loose cascades of harmful effects, even disasters—for example, the DDT used against malaria.

'In Ceylon, in the 1950s the campaign for improved health was massive; the mosquito died, along with other insects; for lack of insects, the lizards perished; for lack of lizards, the cats emigrated; for lack of cats, the rats multiplied, dying now only of hunger and overcrowding; therefore the plague-carrying parasites which infested the rats attacked human beings, who fell back on extermination of the rats, so that the plague became even more widespread. Thousands of cats had to be parachuted on the island in a hurry in order to re-establish the balance.'[1]

The history of the Aswan Dam is also an example of this: the USSR and the USA were competing to 'aid' Egypt to have a source of industrial energy for which this agricultural country had never hitherto felt the need. The dam was built. It interrupted the cycles of the flooding of the Nile valley which for four millenniums had been the source of its riches. It yielded far less energy than had been foreseen because of the evaporation of the water held in behind the dam (head water). It gave rise to the formation down stream of lagoons in which bilharziosis developed, a serious infectious illness which affected the peasants and the fishermen. Lastly, it destroyed the fauna of the delta and of all the Eastern Mediterranean in which the fishing grounds were destroyed. It was a national disaster.

The monocultures imposed upon many of the countries of the Third World by their former colonial powers made them excessively vulnerable to the effects of the economic and monetary crises in Europe, besides which they eliminated the traditional cultures and the indigenous agricultural processes always better suited to the nature of the soil and to the climate.

But, it will be said, the 'technical aid' brought by the Western cultures has nevertheless enabled them or will help them to conquer the ancient fatalities of the poverty of the masses and the periodical famines which, as everyone knows, have for centuries stricken the peoples of India, China and Africa.

But it is the contrary which is becoming the truth. The coming together of the population explosion and the upsetting of the estab-

---

[1] Jérôme Deshusses, *Délivrez Prométhée,* Paris, 1978, from Gordon Rattray Taylor, *The Doomsday Book,* London, 1970.

lished balances, the destruction of forests, too deep tilling, monocultures and mechanisation will soon produce in the Sahel, Biafra, Bangladesh, China and the USSR famines of a magnitude hitherto unknown in the world, which are caused simply by the 'progress' imposed by the Europeans, then by their successors in power in the Third World.

In a general way it is clear that the influence and the activities of the great European companies, superseding the colonising States, are tending to destroy the religious, customary and cultural balances which safeguard come what may the social life in these countries.

One single figure is very revealing about the moral degradation which 'progress' has inflicted upon the Third World: since the end of the last war the International Committee of the Red Cross (IRCC) has been able to visit 300,000 political prisoners in the Third World, which means if one is aware of the obstacles everywhere put in the way of these visits by governments, a total of daily tortures which is not far from the order of size of the Gulag Archipelago.

If it is argued that in spite of these 'blots' Western aid to the Third World is a 'serious' contribution, that is to say economic, financial, technological, *calculable*, we should remember the demonstration made by the most official Agencies that 80% of the aid allocated to the Third World is spent in the donor countries in order to manufacture what is to be 'given'.

All this places upon Europe, the cradle of everything, the onus not only for the material and economic responsibility for the Third World but also for the cultural responsibility, for everything starts there: the crisis as well as the possible solution.

3. No Fertile Agreement With the Third World Without Previous Union Between the Europeans

A *New International Economic Order* is the topic everywhere to be discussed in the intellectual world as well as in that of politics and business. Five or six models have already been proposed to us.

We shall proceed by elimination.

The ecologists, the regionalists and the European federalists reject all notions of productivity without social and cultural brakes; of profitability which crassly ignores the human, social and natural costs; of defence potential which only wants to calculate in megatonnes of explosives—not in the will for autonomy of groups, communities, regions, nations.

They reject the presuppositions of all the nineteenth-century Western models which imply the substitution of the State for the exercise of civic responsibilities, the only guarantees of personal liberties.

They reject the presuppositions of conspicuous waste (a projection of the mad years before 1973) and of the consumption of energy doubling every ten years. They do not want anything to do with a Western model imposing itself on the world by the inexorable logic of unrestricted industrial growth (which is Utopian in the worst meaning of the word). They want, on the contrary, a world society in which *difference* will be not only recognised, but cultivated. They demand the liberty of persons and communities, the one guaranteeing the other.

They know, over and above this, that man can only be free in so far as he is responsible; and he will never be responsible in enormous cities and gigantic collectivities. They want *small units,* social, economic, civic. They want Regions, not Nations. Communities in which the voice of a man can make itself heard so that he can get a reply, engage in a dialogue; something which cannot be done with State-run television services, which speak with a single meaning to passive audiences, that is, to irresponsibles in the etymological meaning of the word: 'incapable of response.'

Those who have undertaken to create the united Europe think that the Western model which today rules the whole world and which is centred on power can only lead to disaster. It must be replaced by a model which aims at liberty. Through the achievement of this other model of Europe alone can our contemporaries be freed from the fascination which the model of power holds over them.

It would serve no good purpose to propose (or worse to try to impose a sort of NIO (New International Order)) even a *European Marshall Plan for the Third World* (a lofty idea) if there did not exist the example of a social interdependent co-operative and libertarian order *achieved* somewhere on earth in our time and preferably in Europe.

Albert Schweitzer said: *'Example is not the best way to influence some one else. It is the only way.'*

The future of a global united order which is the only alternative to economic disaster and to nuclear war is to be found linked to the future of a successful federation of Western Europe.

7

Programme for the Europeans

1. Europe Is Not a Party

We speak of a Programme. But it is not the programme of any party, calling itself European, ecologist, regionalist, federalist, etc.

It is the programme of those who, *in all parties,* see the approach of some dangers and are seeking the same creative replies.

There is, in reality, no good reason why an ecological, regionalist, federalist Europe should become the concern of a single party, thus forcing all the others to declare themselves *against,* simply because they feel that they are excluded or contested *en bloc.* It is certain that among the supporters of all the traditional parties many, possibly the majority, recognise the justice of the ecological, regionalist and federalist theses, even when they are ritualistically condemned by the 'apparatus' of their party—for which, however, they will finally vote out of inertia.

Let the parties continue to exist so long as they have a *raison d'être*: they represent attitudes and mentalities which constitute the sort of language in which they interpret the usual different way to approach the problems which we have tried to define here.

The matter in this Report is one on which all men, the more or less reasonable *and* the informed may unite today in knowledge of cause and in convergence of aims.

2. No One Dares to Confess that He Is Against the Union

The truth is that no one dares to admit openly that he is *for* pollution; dares to say, even if he thinks it, that he is indifferent to the risks of 'excursions' in a Super-Phoenix; or again that he is completely indifferent to the fact that he is leaving to future generations for at least 24,000, probably 120,000, even possibly 5 million years, the daily chore of recooling and isolating thousands of tons of radioactive waste, a permanent threat which through the slightest carelessness may explode in the bowels of the earth and spread deadly clouds over the whole surface of the planet.

No one wants that. We do not want that.

But everyone can see that if we, citizens of the thirty countries of Europe, give a free hand to our disunited States, puerile rivals and all fearful of one another, the worst will become the most probable: indefinitely aggravated economic crisis, inflation and unemployment in twinned growth, genocidal famine, universal endemic terrorism, the whole leading ineluctably to world intercontinental nuclear conflicts which will soon rid nature of her human parasites.

The one grave problem which we are all facing therefore is that of knowing how *to come to a common agreement, in good time, in order to avoid what in any case none of us wants.*

We are not presenting the manifesto of a party which has more than any other the right to call itself European. We are offering concrete propositions, a plan of survival for Europe and for mankind.

3. What Have We Proposed in These Pages?

Let us recall the main trends and sometimes precisely formulated suggestions in the six preceding chapters.

1. *To subordinate the economy no longer to profit but to man.* This could mean, for example: to renounce any enterprise which will be profitable but will cease to be so if one takes into account the social, medico-psychological, war-bearing, environmental, polluting, desert-making and wasteful of natural resources costs and counter-costs. To create continental and regional networks of communication to increase the participation of the citizens in public decisions. Hence: small units of production and stable employment.

   To shorten the hours of work. To improve production with less waste and a more flexible partition of effort. To develop a more autonomous and better diversified agriculture. To bring about a revival of crafts, that is to say the creative leisure time, valorising the resources of the earth.

To plan on a world scale the transfers of technology.

All this presupposes *federal European powers.*

2. To give to the communes and to the regions the right to state their opinion on the sources, the nature and the volume of *Energy,* corresponding to their needs, evaluated by themselves, not by those who sell energy.

   To diminish, then invert the growth rate of energy wastage.

   All this presupposes *European federal powers.*

3. In the service of the Environment, that is of the concern to ensure the equilibrium between Man and Nature:

   To establish a European plan for Water. A plan of salvage of the Mediterranean. The protection of the ozone layer which surrounds the globe. Control of the new chemical products, the fertilisers, the preservatives in food and the universal concreting.

   To this effect, to create *federal Agencies.*

4. To constitute *Regions* and to create their powers, not to 'take' them (they do not exist).

   To stop robbing them of the bulk of their fiscal resources.

   To go beyond the dogma of absolute national sovereignty: to recognise and encourage transfrontier interdependence.

   To set up a *Senate for the Regions,* as the cornerstone of the *European federation.*

5. To stop relying for the *Defence* of Europe on nuclear armaments (offensive by nature) under the command of the Pentagon.

   On the contrary to educate and motivate the will to defend on the spot, local and regional, throughout Europe.

   This demands union, but not of any kind: the *union which expresses itself in the motto 'One for all and all for one'.*

6. To give to the Third World, the example—the only effective one— of a society of a new type, founded on ecological, regionalist and federal principles.

A society aimed not at Power (of the States or of the firms) but the realisation of the people, that is, Liberty.

Only Federated Europe will be able to give this example, on which depends the peace of the world and the continuation of human history.

4. What Will Your Elected Members of Parliament Do About These Proposals?

Usage and rule in a democracy demand that the deputies defend in Parliament the programmes on which they were elected.

It goes without saying that the decisions which will be taken by the European Parliament will be valid within the framework of the powers conferred upon it by the Treaty of Rome, thus that of approving the budget. This, since the beginning of the Western parliaments, has been their main attribution.

The budget speaks the truth (which most speeches betray) about the political will of the community who draw it up in the offices,[1] then discuss it, modify it, accept it finally and then require the executive to conform to it.

To enlarge the powers of Parliament as many demand and some fear would change nothing, since it would not change at all the will of the citizens which in the final analysis is the only thing which counts. (Or then we would no longer be a democracy and any discussion on the powers of Parliament would become a waste of time.)

It would thus be ridiculous to demand beforehand of the future European Parliament that it shall not overstep its powers. This would be to demand in fact that it shall promise, before even being elected, to conform to the minority interests of the political factions in the Community rather than to the will of the voters, alone sovereign in the Community, being so first of all in each of their countries.

---

[1] Example: the governments of the Nine and the Commission of the EEC can make all the speeches they want on the interest, quite particular to them, of the new sources of energy, especially solar energy: when we learn that the budget for 1978 apportions 66 million accounting units to nuclear research against 6 million to research into solar energy, everyone can see at once what they want to do. Who are they? The Commission which proposed the budget, but no less the Parliament which has not modified it on this point.

If the Europeans of the nine countries who are going to elect their Members of Parliament wish to make Europe, they will do so: they will elect a Parliament which will have the mission to find the means for it. If they want this federal Europe—united in respect of its diversities—it will be so.

The only serious question is to know whether they want it, if they have understood that it is the only reply *still* possible to the problems of survival, which are not only economic but moral and even spiritual.

5. Confederation or Federation

Either they have understood that union is vital—or they are going to continue to argue about ineffectual definitions: federation or confederation, for example, which in fact only correspond to the differences in the proportion of sincerity in the decision to unite.

Those who recommend confederation opt for the mistrustful egoistical formula which foresees failure in due course, of the simple liaison: I do not pledge myself to anything over and above what suits me, so much the worse for others.

And those who recommend federation opt for the creative and confident formula of *marriage*: we pledge ourselves reciprocally 'for better or for worse' . . . 'until death do us part', thus without limits of interest or of time.

At last something great, which is at the same time reasonable.

6. You Will Decide

The attitude of the anti-European nationalists of the Right and of the Left seems to us not only immoral but politically comparable to those of Matamore and Gribouille.

It can only lead, at best, to the confirmation of the political satellisation of eight States of Eastern Europe by the USSR, on the one hand, and the placing in economic subcontracting of twenty-two States of Western Europe by the USA, on the other.

We can only escape from this dilemma through continental union, that is by adopting the federal formulae, the only ones which correspond to the true European realities, that is to say to the union not only *in* diversity but *for* the diversity of the Regions. And not only in order to protect them against the annexionist ambitions of an external State but also against the uniformising ambitions of their national capital.

We are not fanatics on the subject of united Europe. We only state that federal union is the only possible solution for the crisis which is rising in each of our countries. We have tried to show the reasons for this to our European compatriots.

Our only aim is to inform on the major problems of Europe the voters of June, the candidates, the ecological, regionalist federalist militants, the national and local elected, some ministers, one or two heads of States, the chroniclers of the mass media who in the short run are the most effective.

There is no question of propaganda. If the facts presented in these pages do not speak clearly enough one cannot see what psychological procedure—advertisement, systematic repetition, pressure, blackmail—could do better in a positive sense. (The dictators know how to do much more, it is true, provided the use of Auschwitz and the Gulag Archipelago.)

This is Europe and the actual facts of its crisis. This could lead to the serfdom or satellisation of our States one by one; or to their renaissance, but all together. The choice is yours. You will have to choose the men and the means which will lead us to one or to the other of these ends: to despair to live in exile from oneself or to the hope of a liberty gained each day, in the personal engagement of every risk.

Victor Hugo wrote a hundred years ago:[1]

'Independently of us the governments try something, but nothing of what they try to do will succeed against your decision, against your liberty, against your sovereignty. Look at them doing it without disquiet, always gently, sometimes with a smile. The supreme future is in you. . . . You are one people, Europe and you desire one thing, Peace.'

---

[1] From Guernsey, 20 August 1878: address to a meeting held in Paris by an English association for peace.

Appendix I

Attitude Towards the Election of the European Parliament[1]

1. Interest in the EEC

From 1973 to 1978 the proportion of those who said that they were *very* interested in the problems of the EEC fell from 24% to 19%.

The proportion of those who were *slightly* interested grew on the other hand from 45% to 51%.

And the proportion of those who had no interest at all remained the same: 26% (no reply 4%).

2. Interest in the Election of the European Parliament

From 1973 to 1978:

For the election, from 54% to 70%.
Against the election, from 23% to 11%.
No reply, from 23% to 19%.

3. Identity: to Remain Oneself

In the EEC, does your country run the risk of losing its culture and its originality?

	B	DK	G	F	IRL	I	L	NL	GB	EC
Yes	24	54	27	22	60	17	45	34	57	31%
No	48	31	58	66	33	70	42	59	36	57%

[1] Source: *Eurobarometer* (ed. by the Commission of the EEC, Brussels), no. 10, January 1979.

4. Solidarity: Willingness to Make Sacrifices for Other Countries

Aspiration towards the solidarity between the member countries and willingness to make personal sacrifices.

	B	DK	G	F	IRL	I	L	NL	GB	EC
Think that the other countries should help (in %) (a)	76	65	63	78	85	94	75	88	70	76
Willing to make personal sacrifices (in %) (b)	28	42	26	37	39	64	34	60	35	41

It is certain that the closer one comes to the date foreseen for the election of the European Parliament at the beginning of June, the more the interest in the election as such will grow, but not necessarily the disposition towards mutual aid.

Looking at the last figures of lines (a) and (b) of the table one concludes that it is not yet established that the Europeans deserve their union.

Appendix II

Inflation and Unemployment

Inflation

Consumer Prices—Price Indices[a] 1975 = 100

	EUR9	D	F	I	NL	B	L	GB	IR	DK
1976 ø	110.9	104.6	109.6	116.7	108.9	109.2	109.8	116.5	117.9	109.0
1977 ø	122.9	108.7	120.0	138.3	116.8	116.9	117.2	135.0	134.0	121.1
1978 ø	132.1	115.5	131.1	155.0	121.2	122.2	120.8	146.1	144.3	133.2

[a]Source: Eurostat 1-1979.

Unemployment

At the end of 1974 in the nine countries of the EEC there was a total of 2.65 million unemployed. At the end of 1976: 5.2 million (double in two years). End of December 1978, the employment offices of the Community had 6.1 million unemployed on their books, that is 5.7% of the active civilian population. (Sweden: 1.8%, Switzerland, 0.3%.)

The provisional average of the number of unemployed registered in the Community was 5,958,000 in 1978. This corresponds to a growth of 3.9% compared with 1977, in which the growth over 1976 was 9.4%.

In 1978 four Member-States registered a temporary drop in their unemployment, but five suffered a growth compared with 1977.

EEC (in %)

Ireland, −7.5; Germany, −3.6; Netherlands, −0.6; United Kingdom, −0.6; Belgium, +8.4; France, +8.9; Italy, +9.9; Luxembourg, +15.5; Denmark, +15.5.

Evolution Towards the Regions

FIRST of all it must be remembered that *federal Germany* was divided by the Allies in 1945 into eleven Länder with the avowed intention of weakening it. In fact, this federalist and regionalist method of government is the explanation for the most part of the 'miracle' of the economic, social and political recovery of the German Federal Republic.

Italy, in 1946 after the downfall of fascism, adopted a constitution which called for the formation of five autonomous regions, which soon became fact: the Val d'Aosta, Sardinia, Sicily, Trentino, Friul and the semi-autonomous regions which only became fact in 1970. The regional method of government has enabled the Communist Party to come to power in several of the large provinces and has thus given the first signs of what a communist non-totalitarian government could be.

Switzerland for nearly 700 years has given the world the example of a federation of historic Regions, which find in the union—strictly limited to certain public functions—the guarantee of their autonomy.

More striking still is the recent evolution of three countries which were forged by the first models of the Nation-State, that is to say, by the grasp of a central and centralising State on the neighbouring countries annexed and aligned regardless of their interests and their cultural, customary and linguistic identities.

In *France,* General de Gaulle was the first to state that the formula for the development of his country was no longer centralisation but the Region. The organisation of 21 'development regions' followed, each grouping some 2 to 7 departments. Several of these regions are doubtful about their size: they wanted it to be 'European', that is competitive with a comparable Land of the GFR, Italian region, or even Swiss canton. It is a beginning.

In *Great Britain,* Scotland elected an already imposing number of autonomist members to the House of Commons, while Wales already has an accredited representative to the Westminster government. The problem of *devolution,* that is to say, of the restitution to the primary nations, annexed in the past or more recently, of their primitive liberties, has become one of the major problems of the United Kingdom, and this evolution is on the whole showing that it favours—with important fits and starts—as the referenda of March 1979 in Scotland and Wales have shown—the growing autonomy of some ethnic regions, some extremists leaders even going so far as to demand the direct attachment of their Region to a united Europe without passing through the London staging-post. But, say the English, 'it is ridiculous to have assemblies for the Scots and for the Welsh and not for the English regions'. This situates the problem on its real level: that of the civic rather than of the ethnic community.

The evolution of *Spain* towards regionalisation after the restoration of the liberal monarchy is exemplary and the best herald for the European future. Against all the sceptics and realists in the rest of Europe, Spain re-instated in fact and in law the autonomy of the government of Catalonia, the *Generalitat.* In 1978 it approved the 'pre-autonomy' of the Basque country (Euzkadi), Galicia, Aragon and the province of Valencia and the Canaries.

Most important, the Constitution adopted in 1978 recognised not only in article 2 *'the right to autonomy of the nationalities and the regions which make up the Spanish nation',* but declares in article 137 that *'the State is composed of communes, provinces and autonomous Communities which will be constituted. All these entities enjoy an autonomy in the management of their respective interests.'*

Lastly, articles 143 to 158 describe in detail the competence and rights of the autonomous communities which are to be created—an exact equivalent of the Regions recommended in Chapter 4 of this Report.

In *Belgium,* a blue-print for a revised Constitution has been in preparation for some years. It makes provision for an allocation of powers between four Regions—Walloon, Flemish, German, and Brussels—but also over and above this division that could have been thought up quite easily in the nineteenth century, it foresees much

Appendix III

more: the allocation of the State power to 'sub-regions' formed by associated communes and which it is proposed to call 'federations of municipalities', of communes, of mini-regions. Never has any constitution of a European country proposed anything so nearly approximating to an integral federalist model.

There remains the decisive case of the *transfrontier Regions.*

The colloquia which met under the auspices of the Council of Europe made it possible to draw up a provisional map of the Regions which are taking shape or are already operational in some sectors.

Some fifteen trans-Rhinal Regions are to be found among them. Five or six are already working, notably *Euregio Nord; Ardennes-Eifel; Moyenne Alsace-Brisgau; Regio basiliensis* (Basle, Baden, Alsace).

The *Lémano-Alpine Region,* studied by the Institut Universitaire d'Etudes Européennes in Geneva, included Suisse-Romande, the Franche-Compté, Savoie, the Val d'Aosta, parts of the Ain and the Isère, sixteen university institutions, two intercontinental airports and 80% of the watchmaking manufacture of the Continent. One part only of this Region, the basin between the Alps and the Jura occupied by the canton of Geneva, Haute-Savoie and the Pays de Gex, enjoys a *Franco-Suisse Commission,* appointed by the governments. Similar institutions have come into force since 1975 in the *Regio basiliensis* and in the *Euregio-Nord.*

The *Alpazur* region (Côte d'Azur, Provinces of Imperia and Cuneo) benefits from the support of all the departmental elected members (French) and provincial elected members (Italians).

The Triestine Region has the unique characteristic of uniting at regional level the subjects of an Eastern country and two Western ones.

Declaration of Copenhagen

Adopted unanimously on 21 September 1978 by the third Convention on the Regionalisation and Decentralisation invited by the Danish Institute:

1. The political organisation of Europe into Regions is the condition of a harmonious and peaceful development of the European peoples.

2. According to the terms of the declaration made in Bordeaux by the Convention of the Council of Europe on the Problems of Regionalisation, terms which we take for our own, the Region in Europe should be defined as the territory of a living community: 'This community is characterised by an historical or cultural, geographic or economic homogeneity, or all these at once together, which gives the population a cohesion in the pursuit of common objectives and interests. It is this cohesion around a number of criteria, which are variable but thought to be essential by the community itself, which gives it its personality and its will to exist and to be seen as a unity.' In no case should regional cutting up establish a frontier across any such community.

3. The Region should enjoy a democratic form of government, with election by universal suffrage to a deliberative Regional Assembly and the existence of a regional executive responsible to it.

4. The principle of regional autonomy applies to all the domains essential for life and the development of the community.

5. The agreements and the conflicts between the Regions, between the Regions and the States, between the Regions and Europe are the object of procedures of concertation and conciliation including, when necessary, recourse to a Court of Arbitrage on the European scale.

6. A second European Chamber, with regional representation, gives to the Regions the means to intervene in the policy of the construction and management of Europe.